TELLING STORIES

.

BRIAN SUMMERALL

TELLING
STORIES

God's Grace Revealed
Through Adventures,
Awkwardness,
and a 1981 Monte Carlo

Whitecaps Media
HOUSTON

Whitecaps Media
Houston, Texas
whitecapsmedia.com

Telling Stories: God's Grace Revealed Through Adventures, Awkwardness, and a 1981 Monte Carlo
© 2018 Brian Summerall
All rights reserved

19 20 21 22 23   6 5 4 3 2

ISBN: 978-1-942732-20-4

For information on bulk purchases of this book, please contact wcm@whitecapsmedia.com

Printed in the United States of America

— To Michele, David, and Daniel —

*I thank God for the story He has written on my life
through each of you. There are many great stories still
ahead, and I'm blessed we get to live them together.*

CONTENTS

· · · · · · · · · · · · · · · · ·

tell·ing *adjective* 1. Having force and producing a striking effect. *verb*. To make known; reveal.

PREFACE
It Started with Snodgrass

· ·

IT STARTED WITH SNODGRASS. Suzy Snodgrass that is. My sophomore English teacher at Richardson High School just outside Dallas. I promise you I did not make up that name, even though it is the equivalent of the teacher in *The Little Rascals* comedies being named "Miss Crabtree."

While we didn't have a Spanky, Alfalfa, or Buckwheat in our class, we did have a very unique cast of characters.

Candy Causey: gorgeous, high school cheerleader, and future Dallas Cowboys cheerleader. I couldn't put together a simple noun-verb-noun sentence whenever she looked my way. When she was near, I usually didn't make eye contact. Instead I stared at the ground, backed away slowly, and hyperventilated into a brown paper bag for the next thirty minutes. Basically, I did the same thing you do when you encounter a bear in the woods.

Scott Sullivan: a six foot five football player who became my best friend in high school. In Miss Snodgrass's class, we sat in alphabetical order. That's how Scott and I met. "Summerall" always came right after "Sullivan" on all our class rolls, until Mimsie Sumner moved in and ruined everything. (No offense, Mimsie.)

Oleg Belinky: a Russian student with a very thick accent. Scott and I suspected he was a spy (it was the eighties, after all). We were convinced we once heard him ask someone, "Excuse for me please, but where for you keep codes for missiles? Thank you very good." We kept our eye on him.

Bjorn Kirchdorfer: another tall one. A six four blond Swede who also became one of my best friends and one of the nicest guys you'll ever meet. (Bjorn's brother was named Ulf. I assumed he was named after the sound his mother made when she had him. Their father's name was Helmut, which must have caused a bit of confusion when organizing sports at family picnics. "Want to play some football, Helmut?")

Then there was me. I think I weighed seventy pounds. I had braces, a mini-fro, bad skin, and was scared to death of girls. Enough said.

It was amongst this cast of characters in that second period sophomore English class that my life changed, and perhaps this book began. Until that point in my life, I never spoke up in class and pretty much kept to myself.

Someone once asked David Letterman if he was the class clown in school. "I wasn't the class clown," he said, "but I wrote for him." That was me. Staying mostly in the background, I might make a comment for the one or two people around me, but I was too shy to go beyond that.

As I mentioned, Scott was six foot five. He sat in the front row on the far left side of the room against the side chalkboard and I sat directly behind him. There I could safely throw out a sarcastic comment and then duck down and hide behind his bulky frame.

One fateful day, I decided that making just Scott and maybe the two people around us laugh was not enough. I went public. Standing up on the seat of my desk, I drew a line from top to bottom on the chalkboard we sat against. Then a few feet down the row I drew another line, creating a column in the middle of the board. From that day on—for two semesters of tenth grade English anyway—that column on the board would be my place to share my thoughts with the world. That three-by-five-foot space on a chalkboard became my very own platform to make people laugh, think, and react. I loved it.

It was my Facebook before there was Facebook. It was before there was an internet or www dot anything. What I might post on my Facebook status today to make my old high school friends laugh are the same types of things I would write on that board daily. It would consist of jokes I had written, comments on current events and the food in the cafeteria, song parodies, and basically anything I thought would amuse my friends. I may have been the first teenager in America to have a place to share my "Status Update."

At first, I called it, "Brian's Bored." (Get it? "Board" vs. "Bored"?) Miss Snodgrass, however, did not appreciate that title, as I don't think she liked the idea of someone being bored in her class. That was the only thing she didn't enjoy, though. She loved it. Miss Snodgrass encouraged me to write. She laughed at everything and asked for more, taking the time to read things to the class I had written that would not fit on the board.

That fantastic woman gave me the confidence to share my thoughts with the world, or at least with anyone who had a class in that room. It was just funny, random stuff, but people started paying attention. I'll never forget one particular day I had started a "Hair for Terry" campaign where I encouraged my fellow students to send their haircut clippings to a fake post office box address to help make a new toupee for Pittsburgh Steelers quarterback Terry Bradshaw (our hometown Dallas Cowboys were mortal enemies of the Steelers). I was standing at my locker and overheard two girls—girls who would never give me the time of day—say, "You'll never believe what he wrote today! I copied it all down for you. Oh my gosh, he's hilarious!" She had written down the fake address I had created. They had no idea I was the author, but it was a thrill to know that what I had written was being read. (I don't think they or anyone else actually sent in any hair clippings, as Mr. Bradshaw's coiffure showed no improvement.)

Writing on that board gave me the courage to speak, even if it was just trivial, fun stuff.

One time, Miss Snodgrass gave the class the option of doing an oral or written book report. I chose the oral report as I thought that would be easier. I thought everyone would want to do an oral report. Turned out I was the only one out of thirty students who did.

Wow, had I made a terrible mistake? Sweating profusely, Afro getting larger from my self-made humidity, I proceeded to walk up to the front of the room in my OP T-shirt, smelling of maximum-strength Clearasil acne cream. After writing "Medieval Update" on the board behind me, I did my best version of Chevy Chase and *Saturday Night Live*'s Weekend Update as if it was broadcast from King Arthur's Court.

Candy Causey laughed. Hard. My life was complete. I could die now. The entire class laughed. A baseball player who sat across from me pulled me aside as I took my seat and said, "Man, I hate book reports, but if you ever do another one, I want to be there."

The unwavering belief Miss Snodgrass had in me, and the encouragement from that crazy cast of characters gave me the courage to try new things. The column on the chalkboard led to a column in the school paper. The oral book reports led to taking the stage in the school talent show and senior play.

When we are fifteen years old, most of our thoughts and observations of the world can comfortably fit in a three-by-five box on a second-period chalkboard. Few things dare venture beyond the white lines.

Things begin to change, though. Life slowly starts to accelerate. The stakes become higher. We grow older and gain more experience. Our life no longer fits in the box.

God begins to color outside the lines. Love and relationships, pain and loss, laughter and tears all start to erase the boundaries drawn on our board. We realize God refuses to let our story and His story be confined to any box.

That's the genesis of this book. In the pages ahead, I tell stories God has given me that don't fit between the lines I had drawn as a teenager. They don't fit in any box or in any particular order. These stories take only a few pages to tell but they reveal a God who can't be contained on even an infinite number of chalkboards. Turn the page for tales of growing up, family, fame, adventure, pain, loss, miracles, relationships, and hopefully humor.

Over my fifty-plus years, it's through these telling and powerful stories that I've found God revealing His truth to me in often wholly unexpected ways. It's my prayer that you will too. At the end of each chapter, you will have the opportunity to reflect and consider a few simple questions about what God may be saying to you.

And Candy Causey, if you are out there reading this, I hope it makes you laugh.

1
World Championship
Water Fighting

· ·

BAYLOR UNIVERSITY, WHERE I ATTENDED COLLEGE, is located in Waco, a small town in central Texas. Now a tourist hotspot thanks to Chip and JoJo, shiplap, demo day, and HGTV, things were vastly different in the early eighties. There was not a heck of a lot to do in Waco then, especially on a late Sunday night. To spice things up a bit, the guys in my freshman dormitory, Penland Hall, invented what we liked to call World Championship Water Fighting.

WCWF, as it was commonly called, consisted of this: taking large buckets of water, large trash cans of water, big cups of water—whatever we could find (this was pre-Super Soaker technology)—and soaking all the guys on the other team, including their rooms and all of their stuff.

On my hall, we would go all out for this. We'd put on our bathing suits, swim shoes, floaties, snorkels, whatever it took. So seriously did we take this event that guys would come from other halls and sit at the end of our hall just to watch us water fight. (At one point in time, there was talk of bleachers being installed. I do think it was on ESPN 8, "The Ocho," for a short while.)

One memorable Sunday night we were in the middle of an over-the-top WCWF. My friend Drex and I were on the same team. Whenever you water fight, you want a guy named Drex on your side. It's not that having Drex on your team would guarantee a win, it's just that with him on your side you knew it was going to be epic. He was this blond surfer-type guy who was on the swim team. He could have been the national poster boy for water fighting. In his dorm room we were gleefully filling up a large trash can full of water, preparing to charge out into the hallway and enter the battle.

The scene is unbelievable. The entire hall is one giant Slip 'N Slide. Guys are zipping down the hall, sliding on their bellies. Water is flying everywhere. It's dripping off the ceiling, running down the tile walls, and standing an inch deep on the carpet. In a word, it is *awesome*.

Drex and I are now positioned at one end of the hall with our colossal trash can full of water. Through all the chaos at the other end of the hallway, we spot a guy standing there. Not only is he perfectly dry, but he is also wearing these perfectly starched khakis along with a perfectly starched button-down shirt along with the cutest little penny loafers you ever did see. He has also made the fatal mistake of having his back to us. As if all of that isn't enough, he has my roommate in a headlock under one arm and my neighbor in a headlock under the other arm, both of whom are on our team!

I look at Drex. Drex looks at me. We look at each other and say, "This can't be." Next, we launch the trash can of water. To this day, I can still see the water cascading in slow motion through the air. The entire volume of water explodes on top of the mystery man, soaking him from head to toe.

Now, most young men would have been satisfied with themselves at this point, but not Drex and me. (Did I mention that this is *world championship* water fighting?) We rush back into the room to refill the trash can to hit him again. The nerve of that guy being dry on our hall on a Sunday night!

We charge back into the battle. I will never forget the feeling or the scene that was now before me.

Everybody had disappeared.

Around forty freshman guys vanished, water buckets and all! There is not a sound. Dead silence in an empty hall. All I can hear is the occasional squish of water under my feet on the carpet and the drip, drip, drip off the ceiling.

Just seconds ago, it was utter mayhem and chaos, water flying everywhere; now only an eerie calm. I had never experienced anything like it. Drex and I look at each other and say, "What in the world just happened?"

Then all of a sudden, my neighbor's door opens just a crack, maybe a quarter of an inch. From inside the darkness, I hear a quiet voice (to this day I don't know who it was) say, "You guys better get out of here. You just soaked the director of all the dorms at Baylor University."

Our hearts sank. We were already on probation for a "previous incident" (I'll tell you about it in another chapter if you promise to keep reading). Baylor was one short step away from throwing us out of school. We were on the Dean's List. Not the one you aspire to, the other one.

In the chaos of doors slamming and everyone running for cover after we soaked him, the dorm director chased and interrogated the wrong guys and we had managed to escape his detection.

Panicked, both of us are thinking, *What are we going to do?* Drex and I run back into his room. Our first brilliant idea consists of running into Drex's closet, closing the door, and turning out the lights. This scheme is quickly nixed. I could just picture us standing in a closet in our soaking-wet bathing suits with a big trash can of water. The door would open, and the director would ask, "What are you guys doing?" and we would, of course, say, "Baptisms—you want one?" (Baylor being a Baptist university and all). It is time we start thinking of a Plan B.

Glancing up on the shelf, I spot Drex's shower caddie where all his toiletries are kept for the community bathrooms. An idea hits me. We lather up our already wet hair with his shampoo and sprint down the hall to the showers. The next forty-five minutes of my life are spent in the shower, lathering, rinsing, and repeating just like the shampoo bottle says. Wrinkled beyond our years, we finally emerge when we think the coast is clear.

Our plan works for a while, but the storm hasn't fully blown over. A manhunt for the culprits has begun. Whoever had the nerve to drench the director of dorms must be captured and brought to swift justice. A hall meeting is called in the study room. The study room is a big room at the end of the hall (perhaps tellingly, none of us have ever been to it before). During the meeting, I try my best to lay low, keeping my head down in the back of the room. I can't help but laugh at the entire scene because the director's glasses keep sliding down his nose since he is still soaking wet, now an hour later.

Responding to my laughter, and obviously irritated, he gets right in my face and yells, "That's OK! I've been wet before!" I honestly was not quite sure how to respond to that, other than to think, *Wow, this guy has really been around.*

Drex and I never broke. No one on our hall snitched. Third Floor North of Penland Hall could not be broken. We shared a bond. We were Water Fighters.

While we became minor celebrities over the days to come as the guys who soaked the dorm director and lived to tell the story, I will never forget, however, that one moment. That surreal feeling of chaos—water flying everywhere—going to calm in just an instant ... just the squish of water under our feet and the drip off the wall.

I've told that story dozens of times over the years. When I first took my oldest son to Baylor, the first place he wanted to see was the door where the voice came from telling us we had soaked the director of dorms and that we needed to get out. Not the football stadium, the live bear mascot on campus, or anything else. Just the place where Drex and I stood and the study room where the meeting was held.

I'm hoping one day there is a plaque there. Preferably a waterproof one.

There are some stories you pass down. Chaos to calm in an instant is not something you see every day, but it has happened before ... on a much larger scale, with much larger stakes, just some two thousand or so years ago. And I have no doubt the guys who were there told this story to all who would listen for years to come. They even wrote it down for us.

"Leaving the crowd, they took [Jesus] along with them in the boat, just as He was; and other boats were with Him. And there arose a fierce gale of wind, and the waves were breaking over the boat so much that the boat was already filling up." (Mark 4:36–37)

Before we fully picture this scene, let's all take a second to throw away our "flannel board Jesus." You know the one. It's the cartoon Jesus you once saw in a Sunday school classroom with butterflies, lambs, and puppy dogs following Him wherever He went. Those pictures just do not do this scene justice.

Make no mistake here, this is not just that the water got choppy, or it started to rain, or it looked a little threatening. It was common on the sea Jesus and His friends were on for tenfoot waves to arise from storms that seemed to come unexpectedly from nowhere. (Take a moment to sit on the floor of the room you are in and look at the wall closest to you. Normally that's ten feet high. Now imagine it's a wave about to crash down on you.)

Waves are breaking over the boat. Friends, when waves break over a boat, people can die. It's that serious. Cue Bon Jovi's "Wanted Dead or Alive" and the opening sequence to the Discovery Channel's *Deadliest Catch*. These guys thought they were done.

"Jesus Himself was in the stern, asleep on the cushion; and they woke Him and said to Him, 'Teacher, do You not care that we are perishing?'" (Mark 4:38)

Have you ever felt that way? Have you ever felt like God is asleep?

"God, where are You? Don't You care what is happening to my family? Don't You care that I just lost one of my best friends? Are You asleep, God? Are You even there?"

If you have felt that way, you are not alone. His very best friends felt that way that day.

"And He got up and rebuked the wind and said to the sea, 'Hush, be still.' And the wind died down and it became perfectly calm." (Mark 4:39)

Chaos—water flying everywhere—to calm in an instant. It doesn't say the storm slightly blew over, or that the water got a little less choppy—it says "completely calm." Chaos to calm at His very word.

I picture the only sound being the squish of water under the feet and the drips falling off their beards as they stood in awe of what they just witnessed.

And then He says to His friends, "Why are you afraid? Do you still have no faith?" (Mark 4:40).

In other words, "Guys, don't you know who's in the boat with you? I made all this stuff. It all belongs to Me. I can tell it to shut up and it will. I can tell it to start again and it will."

Now by this time in their journey with Jesus, they had seen Him do some pretty impressive things. He'd healed some people and done some other great things, but those were mere card tricks compared to telling creation to shut up, and it did.

"They were terrified . . ." (Mark 4:41, NIV 1984)

I picture them suddenly beginning to realize who they're hanging out with and, instead of saying "OMG!" they exclaim, "Oh my You!" (Think about it for a second.)

And they asked each other, "Who is this man, that the wind and the waves obey Him?"

The truth finally begins to penetrate thick skulls. They are not facing the storm alone.

No storm is too large if the Creator is in your boat.

Stop for a minute. Ask yourself, "Is He in my boat?" Or like so many, are you out there navigating the wind and waves on your own. Sadly, too many of us choose to sail alone.

Remember, Mark says that "other boats were with Him."

Some boats chose to go it alone that day. When the storm hit, where did *they* turn?

"Hey Bob, can you do something about this?"

Not so much. Bob may have been a good fisherman, but he had no ability to control the storm raging all around them.

Friends are great. Your talents and skills are valuable. But, none of these will get you "over to the other side." In the first verse of this account, that is what Jesus promised.

"On that day, when evening came, He said to them, 'Let us go over to the other side.'" (Mark 4:35)

He didn't promise there would not be storms. He didn't guarantee it would not be difficult. He just promised He would be with them ("let *us* go over") and that they would make it to the other side together.

In fact, Jesus has never said it would be easy. Quite the opposite (in spite of what the proponents of the "prosperity gospel" might tell you). He promises there will be trouble *but* He will be with us. Those are two things you can count on.

"These things I have spoken to you, so that in Me you may have peace. In the world you have tribulation, but take courage; I have overcome the world." (John 16:33)

"... because God has said, 'Never will I leave you; never will I forsake you.' So we say with confidence, 'The Lord is my helper; I will not be afraid. What can man do to me?'" Hebrews 13:5–6, NIV 1984)

It comes down to these simple rules for life, my friends.

1. When you water fight, you want a guy named Drex on your team, just to make it feel a little more epic.

2. When navigating life, you want Jesus, the Creator, in your boat.

In either case, you weren't made to go it alone.

REFLECTION
....

1. Has there ever been a time in your life when you
   felt like God was asleep? Remember Psalm 121
   the next time you feel that way:

> I will lift up my eyes to the mountains;
> From where shall my help come?
> My help comes from the LORD,
> Who made heaven and earth.
> He will not allow your foot to slip;
> He who keeps you will not slumber.
> Behold, He who keeps Israel
> Will neither slumber nor sleep.
> The LORD is your keeper;
> The LORD is your shade on your right hand.
> The sun will not smite you by day,
> Nor the moon by night.
> The LORD will protect you from all evil;
> He will keep your soul.
> The LORD will guard your going out and
>   your coming in
> From this time forth and forever.
>
>   (Psalm 121)

2. Take inventory of your boat. Who's with you? Is Jesus in your boat as you navigate the storms of life?

3. Have you answered the question in your life that the disciples asked that day: "Who is this man, that the wind and the waves obey Him?"

2
God on the Blanket

. . . .

I HAD LUNCH WITH MY PASTOR THE OTHER DAY. As a child, the very thought of that would have scared the living crud out of me. I grew up in a very formal, liturgical church. My expectation would have been the rector showing up in long flowing robes and a towering hat. Altar boys would lead him through the restaurant (picture Chili's) while swinging those incense thingies, chanting. Surely, he would recite his order in the same way he sang the liturgy of the Eucharist. "I'd like the Oldtimer with cheese and a basket of chips and sal ... sa," he would sing/chant to the bewilderment of our waiter.

As you can see, I could not imagine what a relationship, let alone friendship, with the leader of my church would look like. They all seemed distant, not relatable, and dare I say, not human. I didn't believe he knew anything about my world and struggles. He must have been born and raised on some kind of "Pastor Island" and have a much different DNA makeup than I did. The robes must insulate him from sin while the tall hat made him closer to God than I would ever be.

Thankfully, I outgrew that impression. Lunch with Neal, my pastor, was much different. He wore a T-shirt and jeans. Sporting a golf shirt with a collar, I was overdressed. We walked from the church to Pei Wei. (Always choose your church based on what restaurants are near.) He didn't even use the phrase, "We humbly beseech Thee, therefore . . ." when he asked God to bless the meal.

As we walked, Neal told me why he had missed church the previous Sunday. He and a team of three others had ridden in a bike race called the "Dirty Kanza 200," billed as the "World's Premier Gravel Grinder."

The name alone immediately made me want to take two Advil and a nap. Two hundred miles? I can't drive the hundred or so miles to Waco for a Baylor game without stopping halfway at Dairy Queen for a rest and a Dilly Bar. And that's in a car. Neal and his team each pedalled two hundred miles on bicycles. Yikes.

We discussed the race as we ate. Neal shared about conversations he had with his teammates, some of whom do not know Jesus. The question came up as to whether church members would think it's OK to miss a Sunday to ride in a bike race. Isn't he paid to be there? After all, we are in the middle of a big fundraising campaign for our missions fund. There are a lot of important things going on at the church.

The conversation immediately took my mind to the story of Jesus in the boat that we just looked at in the last chapter, but this time it made me think of a different aspect of it.

"On that day, when evening came, [Jesus] said to them, 'Let us go over to the other side.' Leaving the crowd, they took Him along with them in the boat, just as He was; and other boats were with Him." (Mark 4:35–36)

In the last chapter we looked at the fact that Jesus had power over nature. But in my mind, as awesome and unique as that is, there is an even bigger miracle here than the One who made everything telling it to shut up and it did. After all, it all belongs to Him, as He created it. He *should* be able to do that.

The second miracle—the one that stands out most to me   is that the God of the universe was content to hang out in a boat with twelve guys in the first place. He sought it out. He loved it.

Some might think, "With all the suffering in the world, natural disasters, wars, disease, and starvation, doesn't God have anything better to do? Why is He just hanging out in a boat?"

I know I have asked the same question. However, since I became the father of two boys, I understand the answer to that question just a little bit better. David is our oldest, and five years later my wife Michele gave birth to Daniel.

Before Daniel started walking, he spent a lot of time in our living room on a small, soft blue-and-white-checked baby blanket. He would hang out in his diapers, roll around, play with toys (i.e., put them in his mouth), laugh, and smile at the world going on around him.

When I would come home from work in the late afternoon, that's usually where he would be found.

Now imagine this scenario. Imagine me as Daniel's father, standing above the blanket, looking down at him and asking the following questions:

"Hey, Daniel, what can you tell me about the president's new economic policy?"

"What do you think about global warming?"

"Can you explain to me the internet and its effect on commerce in the global marketplace?"

Comical as it may seem, if I had done that, my sweet son would have just lifted his arms in the air to reach out to me. Tears would soon follow, along with the cry of, "Hold you, Daddy. Hold you."

I could never do that to my boy. It would break my heart. As a loving father, I would not be content to stand above him at a distance, communicating in ways he could not understand.

Instead, when I would come home and find Daniel on the blanket, standing above him or even kneeling down was not enough. I would get down on the blanket and lay down with my boy. I'd tickle him under the chin and whisper in his ear that he is mine. I'd make sure he knew there's nothing he could ever do to make me stop loving him.

Daniel would giggle and laugh when I got down on the blanket with him. We would roll around on the floor and play. When he started talking, he would say, "Love you, Daddy." As he got older he would even say, "I like spending time with you," and I would just melt. Of course, as a loving father who adores my children, I would do that. I'd come down on the blanket to be with my sons.

But, here is even better news. Even if you didn't have an earthly father who would come down on the blanket for you, you have a God who is crazy about you. He was not content to stay above us and communicate in a way that we just could never understand or fully comprehend. The Creator of the universe, your heavenly Father, came "down on the blanket" to be with you.

"[God] became flesh and blood, and moved into the neighborhood." (John 1:14, MSG)

"Behold, a virgin will be with child and bear a son, and she shall call His name Immanuel." (Isaiah 7:14; *Immanuel* means "God with us" in Hebrew.)

His name is not "God at a Distance," "God on a TV Screen," or "God on a Podcast." He is the exact opposite of the gods of the Greeks who did not want to dirty their hands with the lowly, pesky humans. No, God showed up and got His hands dirty. Jesus went to weddings, parties, and dinners; He went fishing with friends and walked along the road with people. He "hung out" (or, as some of my hipper friends would put it, He was a "good hang").

We have a God who came down on the blanket to be with us because He loves us that much. I certainly love the fact that He can tell creation to shut up, but the more miraculous thing to me is His desire to spend time in a boat with twelve guys. He wanted to know them and be known by them.

He desires the same of us.

Yes, there are important things in this world for God to be doing, but none of them is more important than His presence in our life. God with us.

So ride your bike, Neal. Ride it even on Sundays when needed. There will always be things to do at the church, fund-raising campaigns to be completed, and one more sermon to give. But, none of them is more important or a substitute for being with people.

Step into their world and show them the God who did the same for us.

God on the blanket. There's no better place for Him to be.

REFLECTION

....

Think back to your relationship with your father. Consider the images that come to mind. Also, take a moment to take inventory of your relationship with the local church.

1. What adjectives come to mind when thinking about your father?

2. How do those adjectives relate to your image of God?

3. What about your relationship to the church? Do those same adjectives apply?

4. Would you say your relationship to your church is characterized more by television screens and podcasts, or by relationships?

5. If it's not relationships, what steps are you willing to take to change that?

....

"The LORD is near to all who call upon Him, to all who call upon Him in truth." (Psalm 145:18)

"'Am I a God who is near,' declares the LORD, 'and not a God far off?'" (Jeremiah 23:23)

"Draw near to God and He will draw near to you." (James 4:8a)

Remember, if we feel distant from God, it's because *we* moved, not Him. He's been there all along. Come back to the blanket. He can't wait to spend time with you.

3
Raiding the Girls' Dorm

AS I MENTIONED IN AN EARLIER CHAPTER ("World Championship Water Fighting"), there was not a heck of a lot to do at Baylor University in the dorms on a Sunday evening. Before World Championship Water Fighting was invented, we had to come up with something to do on those nights to fill the time.

One particular Sunday night, it was about eleven o'clock, all the guys were sitting around in Penland Hall trying to do anything but study. Suddenly, one guy comes down our hall and says this: "Hey guys! Let's go raid the girls' dorm."

We were so bored he had us at, "Hey guys," but when he added "the girls' dorm" to the equation, we were all in.

There was a girls' dorm known as Collins Hall about three blocks away, and we were convinced that it was six floors of freshmen women who were all waiting to meet us. And like Domino's Pizza, we would deliver.

What you have to understand before we go any further in this story is that in the 1980s at Baylor there was no such thing as a coed dorm. Guys and girls lived in separate buildings and visiting hours were limited to a couple of hours a month on a random Sunday afternoon. We weren't even allowed to have dances on campus during those days.

All excited for our upcoming adventure, we get dressed in sweatshirts, jeans, bandanas on our heads, and sunglasses as our disguise. Just after eleven, fifty guys take off from Penland Hall to make the jog across campus to Collins Hall.

Now it's hard for that many guys wearing sunglasses at almost midnight to look inconspicuous running across campus. The fact that we kept running into trees we couldn't see and falling off curbs we didn't know were there because we were dumb enough to be wearing sunglasses at night didn't help either.

All is going well at first, but just over halfway there, out of the corner of my eye I see this Baylor police car turn the corner and head our way. It looked like our adventure would be over before we got to the Promised Land of Collins Hall.

Quickly I think, *What could we do at this major Baptist university to look inconspicuous so that he'll just pass us by?*

I yell, "Guys! Guys! Get in a circle! Get in a circle!" So everybody gets in a circle.

"Guys! Guys! Join hands! Join hands!" So everybody joins hands.

"Guys! Sit on the lawn! Sit on the lawn!" So we all sit on the lawn, holding hands.

Then I scream at the top of my lungs, "Start singing 'Kumbaya'!"

And all the guys start singing, "Kumbaya, my Lord . . ." and the police car passes us by and the officer must be thinking, *What nice young men those are.*

Danger averted, we get up and continue the journey to Collins Hall. Arriving, we burst in the front doors, into the small reception lobby. It quickly becomes crowded with fifty guys in that tiny space. And there we face . . . the dorm mother.

She's sitting behind a desk, and she looks like she could take all fifty of us. She's got a phone in front of her and is staring at us. All the sudden she starts to reach for the phone. It seemed like it was in slow motion. And then I hear a voice in the crowd of guys exclaim, "Go! Go! Go! Go!" Within a second, fifty guys spread out in every hallway we could find and every elevator we can jump in and every stairwell we can run up and down.

We are all over Collins Hall.

A couple of friends and I burst into the first hallway we could see, and we go running down it screaming at the top of our lungs, banging on all the doors. It was amazing! Girls were opening their doors, grabbing and kissing us, and giving us their phone numbers!

OK, it wasn't like that at all. It was quite the opposite. These ladies *were not* happy to see us. They were screaming, hitting us with anything they could find, and slamming doors. Some were filling cups of scalding hot water from the sink and throwing them on us. It was like World Championship Water Fighting to the DEATH!

I'm beginning to think that this was a horrible idea. (There's no "off" on the genius switch.) It becomes blatantly obvious we have put ourselves in a position we were never meant to be in.

I think we've got to find a way out. So I look down the hall, and I see the big red EXIT sign. So three of us go sprinting down the hall, and we burst out the two exit doors onto a side porch. And then all of the sudden—*boom! boom! boom!*—three spotlights hit us.

Over a PA I hear, "Freeze!" Six police cars are surrounding the exit. It was like an episode of the TV show *Cops*, except we were all wearing shirts.

Your first reaction is not always your best reaction to these panic situations. I leaped off those stairs, and the guys followed me and jumped between the bumpers of the surrounding police cars and sprinted the four blocks back to our dorm.

And of course, we beat the cops, because they were loaded up with donuts and we were nineteen, scared, and fast.

Later that night, we are identified as those who had raided Collins Hall and we are arrested! They don't hold us long, so we're hoping by the next morning the whole thing will blow over. At least we thought that until we read the front page of the next day's Baylor paper.

At first, we thought it was pretty funny that we made the front page of the paper, but then we actually read the article. We were informed there was going to be a disciplinary hearing and they were going to make an example of all of us who were caught (about thirteen of the fifty) and throw us out of school. Dorm raiding would *not* be tolerated at Baylor.

A disciplinary hearing was held, which was covered in the paper as well, and they ended up putting us on probation. While they never threw us out of school, they sure scared the crud out of us.

I will never forget having to pick up the phone and tell the bad news to my dad (who never went to college) that I may get kicked out of school. I had put myself in a situation I was never intended to be in.

Sometimes we are in situations we are never intended to be in. Sometimes we put ourselves in those situations like I did that night at Collins Hall. But sometimes everything's going great, we're where we think we are supposed to be, and those bad situations just seem to find us. And like me in the girls' dorm, we are desperate to find an EXIT sign.

It can come in the form of a phone call that comes out of the blue and informs you there's been an accident. Maybe it's a time when Mom and Dad sit us down and say, "Things aren't working out"—and the rest of life is spent one weekend with one and one weekend with the other because they can't stand to be in the same room anymore. Or maybe it's the doctor that walks into the waiting room and says the test results are not good.

Or maybe, for you, it's like it was for my family. When I was back home from college one summer, there was a knock on our door in the middle of the night. Knocks at the door in the middle of the night are never good. My dad and I both woke up and answered the door. A police officer was there and said to my dad, "Mr. Summerall, your daughter Sharon has been hit by a drunk driver."

She suffered a broken neck. Weeks were spent in the hospital in a "halo device" keeping her neck still. A back and neck brace was worn for months after. Complications from the accident and injury linger to this day.

Like I said, sometimes we find ourselves in situations we were never intended to be in. Sometimes it's because we put ourselves there, but sometimes those situations just know how to find us.

Jesus knows what it's like to be hanging out with friends, everything going well, and those situations just find you. It wasn't from a knock on the door or a phone call that particular day. In this case, bad news came by messenger.

"Now a certain man was sick, Lazarus of Bethany, the village of Mary and her sister Martha. It was the Mary who anointed the Lord with ointment, and wiped His feet with her hair, whose brother Lazarus was sick. So the sisters sent word to Him, saying, 'Lord, behold, he whom You love is sick.'" (John 11:1–3)

Jesus counted Lazarus, Mary, and Martha amongst His best friends.

"So when He heard that he was sick, He then stayed two days longer in the place where He was." (John 11:6)

Strange. It's a bit odd that Jesus got the bad news, yet stayed where He was for two additional days.

"Then after this He said to the disciples, 'Let us go to Judea again.'" (John 11:7)

"So when Jesus came, He found that he had already been in the tomb four days." (John 11:17)

By the time Jesus got the news, waited two days, then traveled back to Judea, Lazarus, His friend, had died and been in the tomb for four days. It appeared Jesus was too late.

"When Mary came where Jesus was, she saw Him, and fell at His feet, saying to Him, 'Lord, if You had been here, my brother would not have died.'" (John 11:32)

In other words, "Hey Jesus, *if only* You wouldn't have dragged Your feet, my brother would be alive!"

We've all got our "if only's"—

- "Hey Jesus, if only my dad were around maybe life would be OK."
- "Hey God, if only I were in a relationship with someone, life would be all right."
- "If only I made a few more dollars …"
- "If only I could lose a few more pounds and look like that magazine cover …"
- "If only I had that job …"
- Hey God. If only … fill in your "if only" here … then life would be OK.

We've all got our "God, if only." The question is, What's yours?

"When Jesus saw her weeping, and the Jews who had come along with her also weeping, he was deeply moved in spirit and troubled." (John 11:33, NIV 1984)

As one of my favorite authors, Max Lucado, has pointed out, Jesus interrupted every funeral He ever went to. It's as if He knew something was terribly wrong, and at funerals, we are in a place we were never intended to be.

"'Come and see, Lord,' they replied.

"Jesus wept." (John 11:34b–35, NIV 1984)

He just broke down. He cried. "Deeply moved in spirit." "Troubled." "Wept." He is overwhelmed.

"So Jesus, again being deeply moved within, came to the tomb. Now it was a cave, and a stone was lying against it. Jesus said, 'Remove the stone.' Martha, the sister of the deceased, said to Him, 'Lord, by this time there will be a stench, for he has been dead four days.'" (John 11:38–39)

In other words, Jesus what are you trying to do? Are you trying to embarrass me? You're too late. He's already decomposing in there. Are you trying to just embarrass my whole family? What are you thinking, Jesus?

Nevertheless, following Jesus' orders, the people took away the stone. "Lazarus, come forth!" Jesus cried out with a loud voice. "The man who had died came forth, bound hand and foot with wrappings, and his face was wrapped around with a cloth. Jesus said to them, 'Unbind him, and let him go'" (John 11:43b–44).

Amazing story. Amazing historical event. But I want to back up. I want to back up to two simple words. The shortest verse in the Bible: "Jesus wept."

Why in the world is Jesus crying? He knows He's about to raise His friend from the dead. He knows they're about to hang out, eat lunch, and have fun like they used to at Lazarus' house with Mary and Martha.

If I know I'm about to raise someone from the dead, I'm not crying. I'm selling T-shirts and funnel cakes, and hiring a band, and saying "Everyone look at me. This is going to be great!"

But, Jesus just breaks down crying. Why in the world is the God of the universe crying when He is about to raise His friend from the dead?

Go back a few more words. The answer is found in the sentence before.

"When Jesus saw her weeping, and the Jews who had come along with her also weeping, he was deeply moved in spirit and troubled." (John 11:33, NIV 1984)

When God looks into our world and He sees the things that we go through that we were never intended to, and He sees the pain and brokenness of our world, it breaks His heart. It hurts Him down to His very soul, causing Him to weep.

We have a God who literally stepped into our pain so that He knows exactly how we feel as we walk through this broken world.

Some of you may be thinking, "You know that sounds really neat and everything, but God doesn't know how *I* feel. Jesus doesn't know how I feel."

You might be thinking, "Brian, I don't know my dad. I haven't seen my dad in forever. Jesus doesn't know what it's like to grow up in a single parent family separated from your earthly father."

Actually, I think He does. Historians believe Joseph died when Jesus was very young, and He knows what it's like to go through life not knowing your earthly father. He does know.

Some may be thinking, "My family just doesn't understand me, Brian. You know I spend as much time as I can at school or at work or other activities to avoid the house. And when I hit the house, I make my way to my room and get on the internet or put headphones on until the next day until I can get out of there again. Home is not a good place to be. Jesus doesn't understand how that feels."

I think He does. Jesus' brothers and sisters by all accounts thought He was nuts. They wanted to have Him committed. Jesus knows exactly what it's like to have a family that doesn't understand you.

Still, some may think, "Well, my family's fine Brian, but it's my friends. I'm just tired of playing the game. When I'm with them everything's great, but as soon as I leave the group or choose to do something different than they do, they're talking about me. They're backstabbing me. Jesus doesn't know what it's like to have a group of friends just totally backstab you and talk about you."

Actually, He does. One of His best friends sold Him out for thirty pieces of silver. "Oh yeah, Jesus, I'm with you. Oh what, thirty piece of silver? He's right there—arrest Him!" Jesus knows exactly what it's like to be backstabbed by a close friend.

And sadly some of you are thinking, "You know what? It would be nice to have friends. The hardest part of life for me is loneliness. I just feel so alone." And you may be thinking Jesus doesn't know what it's like to be lonely.

He does. When He was arrested, all His friends completely deserted Him. He was left all alone. In fact, one of His best friends denied ever meeting Him and cursed His name. The book of Isaiah describes Him as "despised and rejected by men; a man of sorrows, and acquainted with grief" (Isaiah 53:3, ESV). Jesus knows what it's like to be lonely.

Maybe you are like me. Perhaps you suffer from significant anxiety and depression. You know what it's like to have darkness on you that feels like it will never leave. Just getting up in the morning and making it to the shower sometimes takes a Herculean effort. You might think Jesus doesn't know how you feel.

I think He does. On the night He was arrested, Jesus said His soul was "deeply grieved to the point of death" (Mark 14:34). Luke further tells us, "Being in agony He was praying very fervently; and His sweat became like drops of blood, falling upon the ground" (Luke 22:44).

I think it's fair to say that He knows anxiety. He knows depression.

Tragically, some of you reading this book have suffered abuse that's happened to you by the hand of another. Some things have happened to you that only a few know about. And you're thinking, "Jesus has no idea how I feel."

When Jesus was arrested, they took Him, they stripped Him naked, beat Him to a bloody pulp, and they paraded Him around the streets for everyone to point at, laugh at, and mock. Jesus knows exactly what it's like to suffer abuse at the hand of another.

So that when we cry out to God about these things, He's not up there in heaven, saying, "Good luck with all that!"

Instead He's saying to us, "I know. I know."

Yes, sometimes we find ourselves in places we were never intended to be. And whether we put ourselves in those places or those situations find us, God knows exactly how it feels.

You are not alone.

How utterly wonderful that we have a Savior who stepped into our pain. He has felt to the depth of His soul what it feels like to live in a broken world.

He knows.

REFLECTION

....

1. In what way, if any, did your view of Jesus change after reading this chapter?

2. Is there a situation in your life currently which makes you feel like you are at a place where you were never intended to be, and you are looking for the EXIT sign?

3. How does it make you feel to know that Jesus stepped into our pain and can relate to those situations that somehow find all of us?

....

"For we do not have a high priest who cannot sympathize with our weaknesses, but One who has been tempted in all things as we are, yet without sin." (Hebrews 4:15)

4
Pop Goes the Achilles

· ·

FAMILY VACATION. In my youth, that meant our annual pilgrimage to Hilton Head Island in South Carolina. All of my memories of being on Hilton Head are joyous and magical. But getting there, that's another story.

Heading to Hilton Head meant loading up the "family truckster" (a seventies wood-paneled station wagon like in the movie *Vacation*) and driving for two days. My parents were in the front, of course. Our oldest sister, Vicki, got the entire second row seat while Sharon and I, the two youngest, were relegated to lying down in the back "cargo area," along with a large cooler. This was before car seats with NASCAR-like harnesses, as parents were pretty much OK with kids being unrestrained projectiles in the car.

My parents put down a vinyl, padded mat in the back to make it more comfortable. When you fell asleep on it with the summer sun blazing through the untinted windows, it would seal your cheek to the searing hot vinyl next to the pool of drool left by your open mouth. Sharon would have to place her feet on either side of my head and pull me up violently from the pad to break the seal.

Dad was not stopping for anything. The word "McDonald's" was not in his vocabulary. The cooler provided drinks, bread, and lunchmeat. If we grew hungry, Mom was expected to make sandwiches in a speeding car. She was up front with all forms of cutlery, sharpening knives, slicing ham, carving the turkey, and spreading mustard. One quick hit of the brakes and my sisters and I would have quickly formed a Summerall shish kabob, impaled on a carving knife. (If only the highway patrol had a Child Protective Services division!)

Not thoroughly discouraged by those miserable car trips, once I was married and had kids of my own, I continued the tradition of those Hilton Head trips. Thanks to credit card airline miles, though, we avoided the two-day car trip.

It was on one of these vacations that I found myself playing touch football on the beach with family and friends. Desperate for our team to take the lead, I called a classic Nerf Football play. Leaving the huddle with the football stuffed up the back of my shirt to confuse the defense, at the sound of "Hike!" I sprinted toward the corner of the end zone, which I'm sure was marked by a beach towel, Frisbee, or a live crab.

As I ran, from the corner of my eye, I caught a glimpse of my friend, Chris Lipper, rapidly closing in on me. It was now or never if I was going to score. I planted my right foot in a mad effort to leap across the goal line.

Bang! That's exactly what it sounded and felt like.

In a split second, I found myself face down in the sand, experiencing the worst pain I had ever felt in my life. It was as if someone had wildly swung a sledgehammer, landing it squarely on my lower leg. Pain. Excruciating pain.

If you haven't guessed by now or you just dropped this book and retreated to a corner wincing in sympathy pain, I had snapped my Achilles tendon. (Do *not* try this at home!)

As much as it hurt, can I suggest to you that at times like this, pain is a good thing? Pain in the body cries out that something is terribly wrong and desperately needs attention. As I lay there, pain told me that something that was once one, my Achilles, was now two. Separated.

If I could not feel pain in my leg for some reason, perhaps from some nerve damage, then I would not know I had torn my Achilles. I might have kept playing on it, causing further damage. Pain not only let me know something was wrong but also indicated that I needed help.

Face down in the sand, I could do nothing on my own to fix this injury. I needed someone to come from the outside and do something I was not capable of. I needed a great physician who could put back together what I could not. No amount of painkillers or numbing would fix the problem inside me.

Where is this story going? Well, I'd like to suggest to you one more thing. Pain in our world does the same job that pain in our bodies does. It cries out that something is wrong and desperately needs attention. Pain in this context points out that what was intended to be *one* relationally—us and God—is separated relationally and are now two.

"But your iniquities have made a separation between you and your God, and your sins have hidden His face from you so that He does not hear." (Isaiah 59:2)

"But wait," you might think. "Didn't you say back in chapter 2 that He came down on the blanket to be with us?"

Yes, He does love us and came down on the blanket to be with us, but we went in search of other blankets as if there were a better one. We left.

"All we like sheep have gone astray; we have turned every one to his own way." (Isaiah 53:6, ESV)

We look up to God in the midst of the pain in this world and ask, "Why, God, why?" All the while, God looks down to us with a broken heart asking, "Why, Man, why? Why did you leave? You are in a place you were never intended to be, experiencing things you were not made to experience."

The world doesn't work the way it was supposed to.

Let me offer an example of that. I drive a Toyota Highlander, a lovely family SUV. Now the friendly people at Toyota who put my steel blue SUV together piece by piece were kind enough to include a manual with it. This guide tells me what my SUV was made for. It tells me what will cause it good and what will cause it harm.

Now I have a choice. I can toss out the manual and say, "Those people at Toyota just don't know what they are talking about. That book is so old. It was written way back in 2013, and that's a long time ago. They couldn't possibly understand my world. And besides, they are located way over in Japan. That's really far away. The problem is they just don't want me to have any fun."

With that, I could choose to run my SUV on Diet Coke rather than gasoline. As I would go to fill up my SUV with soda, nobody would fly to Texas from Japan to tackle me before I filled the tank. It's my SUV, my choice.

Running on Diet Coke, that SUV will still do some things. The radio might play, and the vehicle will probably make a magnificent fort for the kids, but it will never do all it was created for or go as far as it should.

Sadly, we've all done the same with God. God created us and knitted us together in our mother's womb (Psalm 139). He loves us and left us His Word, which tells us what we were created for. It shows us very clearly what will cause us good and what will cause us harm.

And like everyone else before us, we look at the Bible and say, "That book was written such a long time ago. God couldn't possibly understand my world. And besides, He's so far away. He just doesn't want me to have any fun." Although it breaks

His heart, God won't stop us. By going our own way, we will never experience all we were created for, life to the full.

To make things worse, we try to numb the pain rather than ask what is behind it—our broken relationship with God. Like my Achilles, no amount of numbing will fix the problem that is inside us.

Kurt Cobain was the lead singer for the band Nirvana. At the height of his fame, Cobain committed suicide, shocking the music world that thought he had it all.

After his death, Robert Wilonsky, now editor of the *Dallas Morning News* but then working for another publication, wrote:

> Cobain's death leaves a tremendous gaping hole. Whether you liked Nirvana or not, whether you believe they were our generation's Beatles, this suicide only reinforces the belief that nothing is good enough anymore. Kurt joined a band, got laid, got all the smack he wanted, made a million bucks in one year, got married, had himself a kid, saw the world and it still wasn't enough.

It still wasn't enough to numb the pain.

A great philosopher of our time, Kid Rock (there, I said it), comes to a much better conclusion than Cobain's sad choice of suicide. Reflecting on all he has done to try to numb the pain, he writes:

And I feel like number one
Yet I'm last in line.
I watch my youngest son
And it helps to pass the time.
I take too many pills. It helps to ease the pain.
I made a couple of dollar bills. Still, I feel the same.
Everybody knows my name.
They say it way out loud.
Outstretched hands and one night stands,
Still, I can't find love.
Oh somehow I know there's more to life than this . . .
Only God,
Only God,
Only God knows why.

("Only God Knows Why," by Kid Rock)

Kid Rock wisely turns to God looking for an answer.

God's reply to Kid Rock and all of us? Come home. He sent His Son to take all our sin, hate, lust, prejudice, and injustice and dumped it on Him at the cross. It was enough to kill Him. Ultimate pain.

"This was to fulfill what was spoken through the prophet Isaiah: 'He took up our infirmities and carried our diseases.'" (Matthew 8:17, NIV 1984)

Through His death and resurrection, we are wiped clean of our sins, and He refuses to remember them. Our hearts are mended and restored to a relationship with our Creator. By believing He did this, we can come back to the blanket. Home, without guilt or fear.

"As far as the east is from the west, so far has He removed our transgressions from us." (Psalm 103:12)

"For I will be merciful toward their iniquities, and I will remember their sins no more." (Hebrews 8:12, ESV)

And pain? There will still be pain, serving as a reminder of the broken world we live in. But say "yes" to Jesus, and you won't go through it alone or on your own strength. You'll lean on the One who'll see you through and promises one day to bring it all to an end.

"He will wipe every tear from their eyes. There will be no more death or mourning or crying or pain, for the old order of things has passed away." (Revelation 21:4, NIV 1984)

Stop the numbing. It won't heal you. It can't make two into one again.

Believe. Come back to the blanket. Your heavenly Father is waiting for you there.

REFLECTION

....

Take some time to reflect on things in your own life, currently or in the past, that might signal that something is wrong or needs attention. If that is too personal or painful, take the time to watch the first fifteen minutes of the news tonight. See if any stories scream out that something in this world is broken.

1. If the pain in our lives cries out, then something is wrong and desperately needs attention. Can you name your pain? In other words, what is it in your world that reveals brokenness?

2. What things do you see on the news today that point out the same thing?

3. It's been said that Band-Aids don't cure cancer. With that in mind, what external things do you find yourself doing in your life to try to solve an inner problem? Busyness? A habit? Numbing? Binging on TV? Working harder?

4. After reading this chapter, who is the "Great Physician" and the only One who can heal our inner problem of sin?

....

If and when you find yourself face down in the sand of life, broken, don't fret, don't numb yourself, and don't fear. It's easier than you may think to get an appointment with the Great Physician. He's always accepting new patients.

"Bless the LORD, O my soul, and forget none of His benefits; who pardons all your iniquities, who heals all your diseases." (Psalm 103:2–4)

5
Thank You, Diaper Genie

. . . .

REMEMBER WHEN YOU FIRST DISCOVERED the concept of Halloween? That moment you realized that all you have to do is go door-to-door, knock, say the magic words, and people will give you candy? *There has to be a catch,* you thought. *Does every kid know about this?*

As an adult, there are two other similar times in life. They happen when you get married and when you have kids. It's called "registering."

As a guy, you think, *Let me get this straight. I go to a store, point to things, and then people buy them for me? Is this legal?*

"Great," I tell my betrothed, Michele. "Let's head to the Apple Store, Foot Locker, and Best Buy."

No such luck. Your bride quickly informs you that you will not be heading to stores that carry things that are useful. Instead, you take the escalator up to the third floor of the department store (a place you have never been) and point a laser gun at crystal you will never see again, plates you are not allowed to eat on, and something called "everyday ware." To me, that always meant a pair of shorts, a T-shirt, and a ball cap (oh, maybe that's everyday *wear*).

Your Saturday afternoons are now spent at places like Crate and Barrel, which sells neither crates nor barrels, Pottery Barn, which is not really a barn, Restoration Hardware, which has no cordless drills, and Bed, Bath, and Beyond, where I fear greatly boarding the wrong escalator and falling off into the beyond.

A few years later when we were expecting our first child I thought we would get to register for something fun at Toys R Us. Instead, we wound up at Babies R Us. Babies R Us is the place your tearful wife, who is having trouble breastfeeding your firstborn, sends you ten minutes before it closes to ask the young woman behind the counter, "Excuse me, can you tell me where I can find 'My Breast Friend'?"

So incredibly mortifying.

All of this "registering" culminates at an event called the "Shower." The worst of these is known as the "Couples Shower," which sounds as though it might be illegal in some states. This gathering was created because someone decided that guys were watching too much college football on Saturday afternoons. Surely, we would rather be wearing khakis, eating finger sandwiches, drinking punch, and making small talk. All the while, we get to ooh and ahh as someone unwraps another set of matching his-and-her-dish towels or a solar-powered baby wipe warmer.

Rant over.

At one such gathering, however, Michele and I did receive what I considered to be a magical gift. Friends threw us a couples shower (I'm still uncomfortable with that name) in anticipation of the arrival of our son Daniel. A large box was passed forward to open. Ripping off the paper, I found a fantastic product called the "Diaper Genie" by Playtex (cue awe-inspiring music).

I didn't even know I needed a Diaper Genie until I read the description on the box.

9,600 Dirty Diapers. No, that's not a typo. That's how many diapers the average baby soils in their first three years. Do you really want to trust the job to any brand other than the #1 in diaper disposal?

Ninety-six hundred dirty diapers??? Who can rescue me from this? Tell me more, Diaper Genie.

Three words: Odor. Lock. System. The pail contains a Built-In Odor Controlling Antimicrobial and double airtight clamps to help seal in odors. Good luck getting through that, odors.

Antimicrobial and double airtight clamps? We might just win this war.

What if smells try to get through? Well, that's covered too. The Carbon Filter police will be waiting at the top of the bin to help capture smells that try to sneak out. Moral of the story? A sweeter smelling nursery for baby.

A sweeter smelling nursery for baby? What does the baby care? What about a sweeter smelling house for Dad? These Carbon Filter police need a raise.

I love you, Diaper Genie.

OK, here's the concept. Your baby has a "poopy diaper" (pardon my French). You open the lid of the Diaper Genie, put the dirty diaper inside, twist the lid, close, and the diaper magically disappears! This part is optional, but I would usually add a bow to the device and say, "Thank you, Diaper Genie."

The first week of using this product, I thought it was the greatest thing since a thirty-six-pack of Dr Pepper at Costco. At the end of the week, however, I discovered its dirty little secret: You have to empty the Diaper Genie.

What happened to the Playtex promise of: *If you're lucky enough to own a Diaper Genie, you can forget about taking out the trash and instead concentrate on spending time with your kid.*

Big fat liars.

You can't forget about taking out the trash (unless you are preparing your audition tape for *Hoarders*) because the diapers don't really disappear.

"I trusted you, Diaper Genie! How can I ever give my heart to anyone else and learn to love again???"

It's like finding out your uncle can't really pull an unlimited supply of quarters from your ear or that buffalo wings aren't really chock-full of real buffalo. Sad day. Nevertheless, we used Diaper Genie for all it was worth.

What the Playtex people don't tell you is that Dad is sent in at the end of the week to empty the Diaper Genie. This process begins with my putting on a yellow HAZMAT suit worthy of making blue meth with Walter White on *Breaking Bad*.

Once I create an airtight seal between me and the world, I go in.

Take care to go slowly when opening your Genie. You don't want to make a mess!

Slowly? Not so much. Picture the speed of a NASCAR pit crew. That's me.

Once the back of the Genie is open, what you pull out is something resembling a ten-foot-long chain of sausage links, only instead of delicious sausage, the links are dirty diapers. It easily stretches from one side of the room to the other as you head out to deposit it in the trash.

But, imagine this scenario. What if my son Daniel was old enough to talk and interrupted this process saying, "Dad, I'd like to keep these and decorate my room with them." He then proceeds to string them around the room like Christmas lights.

Finding that just decorating is not enough, my son then drapes the dirty diaper sausage links over his head and wears them around his neck like a long winter scarf that hits the floor.

"This is great! I'm going to wear this around today," he exclaims, beginning to walk out the door, slightly tripping over the excess links spilling down past his feet.

As his loving father, I would hold my nose, look at Daniel and say, "Trust me, son. You were never meant to hold on to those things. And the fact that you are choosing to hold on to those things is causing other people to not want to be around you."

I'd continue. "They're tripping you up, weighing you down, and are dangerous to your health. As your father, I can give you so much better than that, but I can't do that until you choose to put those things down."

As ridiculous as that scenario sounds, sadly it is a picture of us when we decide to hold on to things in our lives that we know we shouldn't. That habit, the relationship, those thoughts, that secret sin.

Even worse, in the world we live in, we often brag about such things and compare the length of the dirty diaper chain around our neck to others. We hold up the diapers one by one to each other, in effect saying, "Look at these words I can say. Look at what I found on the internet. Look what's going on in my relationship. See how I'm cheating my boss. Guess where I was Friday night."

And while the world applauds us for these things (actually celebrates them), God sees them for what they really are. To

Him, we look like a small child with chains of dirty diapers wrapped around our neck and draped around our room.

In other words, we look ridiculous.

As a loving Father, He says to us, "Trust Me. You were never meant to hold on to those things. In fact, choosing to hold on to them is hurting your relationships and isolating you from others. Those things are weighing you down, tripping you up, and hurting your health. I created you, know what you are made for, and can give you so much better, but I can't until you put those things down and turn away from them."

"Repent, then, and turn to God, so that your sins may be wiped out, that times of refreshing may come from the Lord." (Acts 3:19, NIV 1984)

Repentance involves putting things in our life down, turning away from them, and turning to God with open hands. Only when we do that can He fill our life with new things. There are no times of refreshing while holding tightly to old sin.

For some of us, it's time to come to God for the first time, confess that we can't put these things down on our own, and thank Him for sending His Son to die for us. At that point, you are no longer trying to put those things down alone (which always ends in failure and guilt), but you now have the one Person in your life who can help you do something about it.

"Oh, what a miserable person I am! Who will free me from this life that is dominated by sin and death? Thank God! The answer is in Jesus Christ our Lord." (Romans 7:24–25a, NLT)

The same power that raised Jesus from the dead is now in you helping you do things you could never do on your own.

"But if the Spirit of Him who raised Jesus from the dead dwells in you, He who raised Christ Jesus from the dead will also give life to your mortal bodies through His Spirit who dwells in you." (Romans 8:11)

For those of us who have been on this side of the cross for a while, ponder this: What things do you keep going back to from your old life and picking up? You've taken off the dirty diaper sash, but then you go back and pick up parts of it or add new links to the chain. Can you visualize that? Can you see how those things continue to hurt your relationships, trip you up in your walk with Christ, and weigh you down?

We were never meant to hold on to those things! Maybe we need a refresher today in how to put them down.

"Therefore, since we are surrounded by such a great cloud of witnesses, let us throw off everything that hinders and the sin that so easily entangles, and let us run with perseverance the race marked out for us. Let us fix our eyes on Jesus, the author and perfecter of our faith." (Hebrews 12:1–2, NIV 1984)

Take your eyes off the diapers. Fix them instead on Jesus. The more we focus on Him, the more we will see those things for what they are and have the power to put them down.

Remember, you don't need a genie. You need a Savior.

REFLECTION

....

Close your eyes and picture your life before you came into a relationship with Jesus. Get a visual of yourself walking through your everyday life before Him.

1. What things were you holding on to in your life that may have looked good then, but would look like dirty diapers to you now?

2. How did God work in your life and what or who did He use to change your perspective on those things? Was it a process, or did it happen overnight?

3. Where or in what seasons of your life do you find yourself most tempted to go back and pick up those old things?

4. What effect do you think picking up those things and trying to carry them have on your relationship with God? Your relationship with others?

....

Sometimes we think we can't take a relationship with Jesus seriously because we feel we have "too much to give up." If that's you, please realize what you're trading the God who created you for. Just a load of dirty diapers. In other words, a pile of crap.

Worth it?

6
Softball, NASA, and Speech Class

I TOOK SPEECH CLASS THREE TIMES IN HIGH SCHOOL. It wasn't that I failed it. They just kept changing the name of the class, so I was able to take it over and over again and still get credit for it. Thankfully each year the school had a new Speech teacher, so this practice went unnoticed. And I bear no responsibility for running the teacher off each year (as far as you know).

Over three years, I took and received credit for:
- Speech I
- Introduction to Public Speaking
- Speech Communications

I loved it. Standing in front of people speaking was always an enjoyable experience for me. And if you were going to give me academic credit for it, it sure beat sitting in math class.

By my senior year minimal effort was going into my Speech class. Such little effort that I'm afraid it began to wear off on my friends who had not taken the course multiple times like I had. One such friend was Donnie Boyd.

Donnie was a great guy, but on the day our "Informative Speeches" (pick a topic and educate the class on it) it was painfully obvious he had prepared nothing. His topic was NASA's space shuttle program. Knowing there were three students giving speeches before Donnie that morning in class, he and I had a few minutes to huddle in the back row of class to come up with a plan.

Thumbing through one of my textbooks, I noticed a small, colorful brochure the YMCA had left in there about their girls' softball leagues. The school must have let organizations insert these into our books to promote various extracurricular activities.

A plan was hatched! Donnie would go up front and deliver an informative speech about the space shuttle program using the brochure as his notes. He would read from the brochure and each time it said "YMCA" he would say "NASA" and each time it said "softball" he would read "space shuttle."

It worked like a charm. Donnie filled five minutes with that softball brochure. He got an A for his "Space Shuttle Speech."

I guess some things are interchangeable. One speech class can easily be switched for another for credit. And apparently,

NASA and the YMCA can be switched out easily for an A ... at least for a five-minute speech.

We live in a world where one thing can be switched out for another pretty easily.

No Coke? Pepsi is fine. McDonald's for Burger King. Home Depot or Lowe's. Chevy for Ford. Pizza Hut for Dominoes. Chick-fil-A for ... (OK, every analogy breaks down somewhere—nothing substitutes for Chick-fil-A!)

Hopefully, you get my point. In some cases, there's not just one right answer.

In other areas of life, however, that's not the case. Notice what God's Word says: "There is but *one* God, the Father, from whom are all things and we exist for Him; and *one* Lord, Jesus Christ, by whom are all things, and we exist through Him." (1 Corinthians 8:6, emphasis added)

When it comes to God, there is only one answer. You can't spin the "wheel of gods" and just settle for whatever it lands on. There is only one God who is not to be switched out, YMCA/NASA-style, with anyone or anything.

Now I know that's not a popular view. We live in a world that doesn't want to say anyone is "wrong." Everything is relative, and everyone gets a trophy.

That may be the current wisdom of man, but God's Word seems to be very clear.

"For there is one God, and one mediator also between God and men, the man Christ Jesus." (1 Timothy 2:5)

"Thus says the LORD, the King of Israel and his Redeemer, the LORD of hosts: 'I am the first and I am the last, and there is no God besides Me.'" (Isaiah 44:6)

"I, even I, am the LORD, and there is no savior besides Me." (Isaiah 43:11)

If anyone should have understood this in all of history, you would think it would have been the Israelites. They were God's chosen people. He parted the Red Sea for them, led them with a pillar of cloud by day and fire by night, and provided manna each morning.

Yet, in spite of experiencing His deliverance again and again, they chose the any-god-will-do option.

"Then the sons of Israel did evil in the sight of the LORD, served the Baals and the Ashtaroth, the gods of Aram, the gods of Sidon, the gods of Moab, the gods of the sons of Ammon, and the gods of the Philistines." (Judges 10:6)

In other words, "Why serve one God when we can have seven? Any one good answer is as good as another. Besides, we don't offend anyone."

Before we are too hard on the Israelites I have to admit I do the same thing. God has delivered me, He sent His Son to die for my sin, and offers me a relationship with Him. He has provided me with blessing beyond anything I will ever deserve.

But just like the Israelites, I think, *Surely I need more than just Him. What's wrong with adding a few other options?* Maybe

I don't go so far as to add Baal to the equation, but I add my own options to spinning the "wheel of gods":

- Money
- Success
- Comfort
- Popularity
- Ego
- Material Things
- Pleasure

There's just seven off the top of my head that I pull the YMCA/NASA switch for. Take out God and add any one of those things that I look to find fulfillment in. My false gods may not have fancy names like the ones the Israelites turned to or sound as menacing, but the result is the same.

And while we "don't want to offend anyone" by saying there is only one answer, *God* is offended.

"They forsook the LORD and did not serve Him. The anger of the LORD burned against Israel." (Judges 10:6–7)

"The LORD said to the sons of Israel, 'Did I not deliver you from the Egyptians, the Amorites, the sons of Ammon, and the Philistines? Also when the Sidonians, the Amalekites and the Maonites oppressed you, you cried out to Me, and I delivered you from their hands. Yet you have forsaken Me and served other gods; therefore I will no longer deliver you. Go and cry out to the gods which you have chosen; let them deliver you in the time of your distress." (Judges 10:11–14)

That's just it. While those things I trade for God may provide temporary relief or the momentary applause of men, none of those things can save me.

And that is what I am in desperate need of: a Savior.

Jesus told us, "I am the way, and the truth, and the life; no one comes to the Father but through Me" (John 14:6).

And Peter reminds us, "There is salvation in no one else, for there is no other name under heaven given among men by which we must be saved" (Acts 4:12, ESV).

One way. One answer.

To some that may seem unfair or too narrow. Try to picture it this way:

You work in an office building with only one exit (go with me on this one). The designer/creator/owner of that building comes into your work and gives an informative lecture on fire safety and how to get out of the exit in case of emergency. He takes time to explain that this single exit is available to all and sufficient.

After the lecture, he leaves. Immediately the employees begin to laugh and call him a jerk. "The nerve of him telling us there is only one way out of this building! What a jerk! There are many ways out! We know better than that so-called creator!"

Not only that, but each employee begins to think his fire safety tips were just trying to impinge on their personal freedom. As ridiculous as it sounds, they start lighting matches and laughingly tossing them in all the trash cans and recycling bins.

Within minutes, a fire starts. Employees, out of pride, rush around to find any exit except the "narrow way" that the creator of the building pointed them to. Many perish.

As he is driving away, the creator of the building notices the smoke and rushes back to the site. He and his only son, who happens to be with him, rush into the building to save everyone they can. Six employees are saved, while ten others don't make it out. In the process, his only son is killed during the rescue.

What would the headline read the next day?

SELFISH JERK LEAVES 10 TO PERISH

Or would it read ...

SELFLESS HERO SAVES 6,

LOSES SON IN COURAGEOUS EFFORT

TO SAVE LOST EMPLOYEES

WHO FAILED TO HEED WARNINGS

I think the second is far more accurate.

Like the designer of the building, God made all of creation and us. We turned our back on Him and exchanged Him for other "gods." In spite of our rebellion, He returned in the form of His Son, Jesus, and paid the price for our sin. God's salvation plan is freely available to everyone.

I may have gotten credit for three different Speech classes, and Donnie might have gotten an A on his speech, but God's passing grade comes through only one name, Jesus, freely given and available to all.

REFLECTION

....

1. What are the things in your life that you "trade out" for God?

2. As you have grown older, have those things changed in your life?

3. Why do you think we are so quick to let other things take His place, even after we know Him?

4. When those things let you down, how quick are you to turn back to God?

....

"Now return to the LORD your God, for He is gracious and compassionate, slow to anger, abounding in lovingkindness and relenting of evil." (Joel 2:13)

"'Return to Me,' declares the LORD of hosts, 'that I may return to you.'" (Zechariah 1:3)

"If you return to the Almighty, you will be restored . . ." (Job 22:23)

7
Run Faster!!!

IF YOU EVER HAVE KIDS, it won't take long for you to discover the "joys" of organized sports. Now don't get me wrong, our oldest, David, played baseball from kindergarten to sixth grade and had a blast doing it. Practice was once a week, and whose house you swam at after the game was more important than winning or losing.

I wish our second child, Daniel, had been afforded the same experience. I should have known things were going to be different with his class when at the fall pre-kindergarten picnic I overheard the dads sizing up each kid for the football team. Apparently, they scout early around here.

Spring brought T-ball. The first week of the season, the parents got together and hired an ex-Texas Ranger (as in the professional baseball team, not the legendary law enforcement agency) to be our hitting coach. Did I mention these kids were five and hitting a ball off a tee? I had no clue that college scouts were now hitting the T-ball leagues.

While David's experience was more laid back than Daniel's, not everyone shared that casual attitude. I'll never forget one particular first-grade soccer game I attended. The parent of one of David's teammates was sitting in a nice, comfortable lawn chair on the sidelines. This particular boy was a great little athlete, always giving it everything he had, and in fact was far and away one of the best players on the field. Yet as the boy would run down the field, any time he got within twenty yards of his father the dad would berate him at the top of his lungs, yelling, "Run faster!!!"

It wasn't just a one time thing. *Every time* the little boy passed, we were all treated to a disapproving father screaming at his son, "Run faster! Run faster!"

Finally, the son had enough. Fed up with the criticism of the one sitting comfortably in a chair, the next time the six-year-old ran by the sideline and his father, he threw out his arms in exasperation and yelled back, *"I'm running as fast as I can!!!"*

Mic drop.

Dad didn't yell again.

I wonder how many times I have made the mistake of picturing God as the father on the sidelines of that soccer game. Before I knew Jesus, my image of God was of a father far removed from us in the stands of heaven, thoroughly dissatisfied with my efforts, imploring me to do better, try harder, do more!

Even after beginning a relationship with Jesus, I can see where I often fall into the same trap. I picture myself out on the field of life trying my best to serve Him, do ministry, and live my life according to His will. And what voice do I think I hear from the stands of heaven? It's the disapproving voice of a father yelling, "Run faster!!!"

Or more specifically, "Have more quiet times! Be good! Give more! Go to more Bible studies! Listen to more Christian podcasts! You're just not doing enough! Put another fish magnet on your minivan! Wear more cheesy Christian T-shirts! (OK, maybe not the last two, but you get the idea.)

All the while, I am looking up to God trying my best to do my Christian "song and dance," and I'm thinking, *I'm running as fast as I can!*

The only problem with this way of life is that the voice I am answering to is not the Lord's. It's a lie. God's voice is not the same as my earthly father I tried so hard to please with straight A's every semester, or the disapproving dad in the lawn chair on the sidelines.

Want to know what He is really saying? Put away the lies for just a minute, stop looking to the imaginary sidelines, and listen to the voice of your real Father.

"For thus the Lord GOD, the Holy One of Israel, has said, 'In repentance and rest you will be saved, in quietness and trust is your strength.'" (Isaiah 30:15)

"Be still before the LORD and wait patiently for him; do not fret." (Psalm 37:7, NIV 1984)

"Slow down. Take a deep breath. What's the hurry? Why wear yourself out? Just what are you after anyway?" (Jeremiah 2:25, MSG)

God's voice is the opposite of the voice on the sideline yelling, "Run faster!!!" And remember, He's never been content to be on the sidelines, so it's definitely *not* His voice if that is where you hear it from.

"The LORD your God is *with* you, he is mighty to save. He will take great delight in you, he will quiet you with his love, he will rejoice over you with singing." (Zephaniah 3:17, NIV 1984, emphasis added)

He's "God with you, Immanuel," not God disapprovingly sitting on the sidelines in a camping chair. The one who holds the oceans in the palm of His hand can't be confined to a lawn chair, my friends.

If it's not Him yelling, "Run faster!" then who is it? Don't forget, you have an enemy. An enemy who wants you to feel defeated and unworthy, and desperately wants you to give up.

"Be sober-minded; be watchful. Your adversary the devil prowls around like a roaring lion, seeking someone to devour." (1 Peter 5:8, ESV)

"But I am afraid that just as Eve was deceived by the serpent's cunning, your minds may somehow be led astray from your sincere and pure devotion to Christ." (2 Corinthians 11:3, NIV 1984)

When you hear the "Run faster!" voice, call it what it is. A lie. Deception from your enemy who is trying to lead you astray "from your sincere and pure devotion to Christ." It's just plain garbage.

What happens when that voice comes from other believers? Call it the same. Garbage.

Sometimes even those who claim to know Jesus will tell you that you're just not doing it right. But be of good cheer. They said the same to Jesus. Remember when He had dinner with the tax collector, Zacchaeus, and hung out with his friends? Surely, they thought, the Savior had more pressing work to do and more important people to meet.

"When they saw it, they all began to grumble, saying, 'He has gone to be the guest of a man who is a sinner.'" (Luke 19:7)

Bill Starr, former president of Young Life, puts it this way,

Notice the response of those who are standing by [on the sidelines], those who are not involved in reaching out, or

extending a hand to reach another ... From the very beginning of Christ expressing his mission from the Father, he is
criticized. He never does it "right." The activity in which he
is engaged, the matter in which he does it, all seem wrong
when measured by what the cultural standard says is right.

It's a given. Some people just won't like the way you do
it. That's OK. Remember, when that happens, you're in good
company.

Stop playing the comparison game. And when your enemy
or even a fellow believer lobs a "Run faster!" lie your way,
instead of throwing out your arms in exasperation, just pass
those lawn chairs by. Let the voice of your Creator be your
compass.

"Be still, and know that I am God." (Psalm 46:10, ESV)

"Come to Me, all who are weary and heavy-laden, and I
will give you rest. Take My yoke upon you and learn from
Me, for I am gentle and humble in heart, and you will find rest
for your souls. For My yoke is easy and My burden is light."
(Matthew 11:28–30)

The loudmouth critic in the lawn chair (whose yoke is anything but easy) doesn't get a vote. In the words of Theodore
Roosevelt,

It is not the critic who counts; not the man who points out
how the strong man stumbles, or where the doer of deeds

could have done them better. The credit belongs to the man who is actually in the arena ... who knows great enthusiasms, the great devotions; who spends himself in a worthy cause ... so that his place shall never be with those cold and timid souls who neither know victory nor defeat.

REFLECTION
....

1. When it comes to your spiritual life, have you ever felt like you heard the words, "Run faster!!!"?

2. Did you hear those voices in your own head? From other believers? Where did they come from?

3. What do you think God would like to say to you during those times?

4. Has your own personal salvation ever actually been dependent on your "trying harder"? (Remember Ephesians 2:8–9: "For by grace you have been saved through faith; and that not of yourselves, it is the gift of God.")

....

If you are surprised you have enemies, don't be discouraged. It means you are making a difference!

8
Turn Up the Volume

. . . .

STARTED IN DALLAS IN 1941, Young Life is an outreach ministry
to adolescents which is now found in over a hundred countries.
I was first exposed to Young Life at Baylor through a good
friend, and was quickly taken by founder Jim Rayburn's phi-
losophy that, as he put it, "if you want kids to go to Sunday
school, don't have it on Sunday and don't call it school."
Rayburn further explained, "Christ is the strongest, grand-
est, most attractive personality ever to grace the earth. But a
careless messenger with the wrong method can reduce all this
magnificence to the level of boredom ... It is a crime to bore
anyone with the gospel."

I fell in love with this ministry and its relational approach to
sharing Christ. Volunteering in Waco during my college years

in a local high school club, upon graduation I went on Young Life staff full-time (and have now been on staff for over thirty years!).

Laura was one of my Young Life kids back in my early ministry days. She was quite the character. Smile on her face, bright eyes, and always quick with a laugh.

While she excelled at many things, driving was a bit of a different story. When she left for college in Oklahoma, she became a part of a group of my former Young Life kids that would meet up for church whenever they were back in town for the weekend. A lunch full of college stories always followed.

This particular lunch, Laura told of a horrible noise her car made all the way back home to Dallas from OU. I asked if she stopped to find out what it was. I'll never forget her response.

She said, "No, but if I turned up the radio really loud, I couldn't hear it."

Turns out she had a broken axle. Turning up the volume does not fix a broken axle.

A month later she is back in town, axle fixed. She begins to tell the story of how all the bridges iced over in Oklahoma the week before. She was approaching one in her car and a police officer was standing in front of the bridge with his hands up to slow and stop any approaching vehicles.

Laura panicked and slammed on her brakes. Her car tried to stop but began sliding on the ice at an alarming rate of speed. She was heading right for the police officer.

Believing she would stop, he stood his ground, hands up.

Bam! She hit him. Stunned, his hands and chest hit the front of her car. Angered, he began screaming at her to stop and pounded his fist on the hood. Meanwhile, his feet were sliding backward on the ice.

Slowly the car overtook him as he lost his grip on the hood … then the hood ornament … then the front bumper. The vehicle continued to slide as he was now entirely under it, sliding on his back, holding on to anything he could grab.

The car finally comes to a stop, and thankfully the unfortunate officer was not hurt, just scraped up a bit. Laura claimed, "The whole time I could hear him from under the car's floorboard, yelling at me."

"But if you turned up the radio, you couldn't hear him," I replied. (This might be a good time to point out the fact that the words "compassionate," "pastoral," and "counselor" have never shown up on my Strength Finders test results … but you may have already figured that out by this chapter.)

In all seriousness, I am exactly like Laura. Not so much when it comes to cars and driving, but definitely when it comes to turning up the noise in my life.

I fall asleep with earbuds in my ears listening to the latest podcast. At least three different "shower radios" have been purchased in my lifetime. I drive a four-door car that has twelve speakers in it. Bose headphones are in my backpack, currently six feet away from me on the couch. Three feet away from me on my desk is my iHome radio playing sports radio. I often sleep with a "white noise" machine.

Sound like a man with a problem? It's as if I fear silence.

I don't think I am alone. It's not just audio noise either. It's visual noise as well. I've checked Facebook twice since I started writing these last two paragraphs.

Have you ever stood in the middle of Times Square in New York City at night? The amount of messages coming at you at once—video screens, billboards, people yelling, cars honking—is overwhelming. Times Square in exciting, to be sure, but you wouldn't want to live there or raise your kids in the middle of it. Yet it's as if every morning I park my brain dead smack in the middle of Times Square. Surrounded by noise and screens, warning sounds of the "broken axles" of my life and the people I may be figuratively "running over" are blocked out.

The message is, "Don't stop moving. Don't slow down. Whatever you do, don't pull over to see if anything is wrong. Just turn up the noise!"

I've left no room for silence. But it's often in the silence that God speaks.

In the book of 1 Kings, the prophet Elijah is discouraged to the point that he is praying to the Lord to take his life.

"He came to a broom tree, sat down under it and prayed that he might die. 'I have had enough, LORD,' he said. 'Take my life; I am no better than my ancestors.'" (1 Kings 19:4b, NIV 1984)

Looking at the recent headlines, Elijah is not the only person who has felt this way. Suicide seems to be rampant. Over the last couple of years comedian Robin Williams, designer Kate Spade, celebrity chef Anthony Bourdain, lead singer of Linkin Park Chester Bennington ... all came to the point where they said, "I have had enough."

Thankfully, Elijah's story does not end there.

"The LORD said, 'Go out and stand on the mountain in the presence of the LORD, for the LORD is about to pass by.'

"Then a great and powerful wind tore the mountains apart and shattered the rocks before the LORD, but the LORD was not in the wind. After the wind there was an earthquake, but the LORD was not in the earthquake. After the earthquake came a fire, but the LORD was not in the fire." (1 Kings 19:11–12a, NIV 1984)

Wind, Earthquake, and Fire (one of my favorite seventies groups), but the Lord was not in any of the loud, flashy things.

"And after the fire came a gentle whisper. When Elijah heard it, he pulled his cloak over his face and went out and stood at the mouth of the cave.

"Then a voice said to him, 'What are you doing here, Elijah?'" (1 Kings 19:12b–13)

God's voice to the one who was ready to give up came as a "gentle whisper."

If God's voice comes as a gentle whisper, how will I ever hear it in the midst of my life of noise? Turning up the volume tunes out God's voice just like turning up the radio drowned out the broken axle.

I am the worst at this, but let me challenge both you and me to a few things that might just allow us to hear God's voice on a daily basis.

- No looking at your phone or email until thirty minutes after you get up or thirty minutes before you go to bed.
- Don't turn on the car radio until ten minutes into your drive.
- It's OK to walk into the living room without turning on the television.
- Throw the shower/bathroom radio in the trash.

In other words, don't fear the silence. I'll try it if you will. Leave room for God to speak. Put yourself in a position to listen. You might be surprised what you hear.

I didn't find out until years later, but Laura came to a point in high school where merely turning up the radio would not drown out all the things that were wrong in her life. She wrote me this letter before graduating from college.

My senior year in high school I went through a phase where things went from bad to worse, and nothing was going right. I eventually lost hope that anything would change. For the first time in my life, I started thinking about suicide.

I decided that I was going to kill myself because anything had to be better than things were going at the time. I even had a plan.

Like Elijah, Robin Williams, Kate Spade, Anthony Bourdain, and countless others, Laura had had enough. All the car radios in the world could not drown out the broken axle pain in her life.

I was going to go to school on Monday, be as happy as I could, spend the afternoon with my brother, and go to Young Life that night. Tuesday I was going to go through with my plan.

Elijah went to the woods and a cave for a break from the noise and found God. Laura went to Young Life.

I went to Young Life that Monday night and totally freaked out because you were talking about suicide. This scared me bad enough that I really listened. I realized God would help me through everything if I let Him. More importantly, for the first time in a long while, I actually felt how much He LOVED ME!

In the midst of the craziness and busyness of high school, Laura, like Elijah, put herself in a place where she could hear and experience God's love. And it changed her path forever. She's now a teacher, married to a wonderful man, and I love keeping up with her smiling face on Facebook.

Elijah found a cave. Laura found a Young Life club. Where is your place? Where will you slow down, pull over from the craziness, turn down the radio, and listen for His voice?

If you do, like Elijah you might find out you are not alone. Like Laura, you might begin to feel how much He LOVES YOU. You have never left His sight, and He has a plan for you beyond your current circumstances.

"'For I know the plans that I have for you,' declares the LORD, 'plans for welfare and not for calamity to give you a future and a hope.'" (Jeremiah 29:11)

Now *that's* worth turning down the radio for.

REFLECTION
....

1. Take inventory of your life. Where do you experience silence?

2. What are some things in your life that keep you from experiencing silence? Are they necessary? Can they be eliminated?

3. Like the cave for Elijah or Young Life for Laura, do you have a place where you can go on a regular basis to hear the whisper of God's voice?

4. If it's not in your house but instead some other place, make a plan to go there this week and spend some time. Ask someone close to you to hold you accountable.

....

And if on your way there, a bridge is out due to ice, don't slam your brakes too hard. The cop guarding the bridge will thank you.

9
Living it Up at the Hotel California
. . . .

SCENE: A HIGH SCHOOL BOY'S ROOM. Posters on the wall. Door closed. Panasonic stereo blaring (record player, built-in AM/FM tuner, and this newfangled thing called a cassette deck).

A sixteen-year-old is playing air guitar to the Eagles' "Life in the Fast Lane" and lip-syncing to an imaginary crowd. Later, he'll settle the crowd down for the final encore with his lip-sync of "Desperado." He dazzles them with his air "key-tar" on this number. So versatile. Mom calls that dinner is ready. Concert ends. Second show after dinner. He'll lip-sync all four parts of the a cappella harmonies of "Seven Bridges Road" at once. A lesser man might pull a muscle.

That boy was me. As a high school kid, I loved the Eagles. I grew up on them. "Hotel California," "Take it Easy," "Tequila Sunrise," "Lyin' Eyes," "Heartache Tonight" ... they were the soundtrack of my life. OK, other people's lives, as I weighed under a buck, had never been on a date, and was forced by my dad to play golf wearing Izod shirts and matching shorts daily at the country club. Life in the school zone, surely make you lose your mind.

I knew everything about the Eagles. I knew they started at the Troubadour Club in Los Angeles, a city I dreamed of living in one day. I knew that Don Henley and Glenn Frey were the brains behind the operation, and they had met as the backing band for Linda Ronstadt. On that Panasonic stereo, I wore out *Eagles Greatest Hits 1971–1975* (the best-selling album of all time in the U.S., by the way). I remember purchasing *The Long Run* album from Sound Town (love that name) and stealing *Hotel California* from my sister Sharon whenever she wasn't looking.

When the Eagles broke up, I followed Don Henley. Sure, I bought Glenn Frey's solo stuff, but Henley was the one I wanted to be and knew everything about. He grew up in Linden, Texas. His mom was a school teacher. He majored in English at the University of North Texas.

I stopped at Sound Warehouse (Sound Town had closed) at the corner of Belt Line and Preston and bought my *End of the Innocence* cassette tape as I prepared to drive to Colorado to work at a Young Life summer camp in college. All the way to Colorado in my red Nissan 200SX, sunroof open, I played and replayed it so many times it probably stretched the tape. Each lyric was meticulously memorized and analyzed.

Fast forward a few years (cassette metaphor). While working at another Young Life camp for the summer in North Carolina, I get a message in my box that says, "Brian, your sister is going out on a blind date with Don Henley." I immediately think, "*I* should be going out on a blind date with Don Henley! Sharon knows nothing about him!"

The next thing I know, my sister is dating Don Henley. About a year or so later, Don leans over to me at dinner and says, "We want you to be a groomsman in our wedding." Before I know it, I'm standing on what used to be Barbra Streisand's ranch in Malibu, California, and I am a groomsman in Don Henley's wedding. Sure, my sister was there, *but this was Don Henley's wedding!*

One Los Angeles newspaper called the reception the "Rock Concert of the Decade." Don, Bruce Springsteen, Billy Joel, Sheryl Crow, Sting, Jackson Browne, Glenn Frey, and John Fogerty all took turns with the band. Tony Bennett did a thirty-minute set to honor my parents. It was surreal.

Across the dance floor from my table, I could see Jack Nicholson and his table. He had his sunglasses on. Inside. At night. So cool. As I scanned the room, I saw Courtney Cox, Jimmy Buffet, and Ben Stiller. The list went on and on. At 2:00

in the morning, I was a part of four couples out on the dance floor, dancing in a small group circle like you would at your high school homecoming dance. Only this time it was me and one of the bridesmaids, Bruce Springsteen and his wife, Bob Seeger and his wife, and Bruce Hornsby and his wife. (If you are a millennial, trust me, they are "Dad Rock" famous.)

It was as if I had won some "Rock and Roll Fantasy Prom" contest by writing an essay for a local radio station. "Little Brian Summerall from Richardson, Texas, writes in ..."

Looking back, I realize that all of my "head knowledge" of Don Henley would never have gotten me into the room that night. (Believe me, there was *plenty* of security everywhere.) I could have walked up to any door and quoted my trivia ... "Best selling album of all time; his first band was named Shilo; Dad sold auto parts." They would have looked at me and said, "He doesn't know you."

I could have run into Don Henley on the street and said, "You were born in Linden, Grammys for 'End of the Innocence' and 'Boys of Summer,' discovered by country singer, Kenny Rogers." He would have looked at me and said, "Do I know you?" My reply would have been, "No, but I know everything about you."

As the police were dragging me off and restraining orders were being filed, I would have realized that there is a big difference between knowing all about someone and actually knowing them, having an actual relationship.

There are benefits, too. When my family would go to an Eagles concert, we wouldn't go online and hope to get tickets. We traveled with the band ... and it was very cool. A van would pull up to Don's house or hotel, and we'd all load up. A police escort would lead us to the stadium. What was really fun was taking my own car and following. I got the police escort as well. We'd speed, go the wrong way down one-way streets, run red lights—all with motorcycle cops with lights flashing on either side of the cars. It was like being a president. Imagine my grin of glee as I drove.

Pulling up under the arena or stadium, Don would always have a hospitality room filled with the best barbecue or Tex-Mex. I'd load up my plate, and if anyone asked what I was doing, I could point over to Don and say, "I'm with him," and they'd say, "Take anything you want." And I did. I'd line my pockets with ziplock bags and aluminum foil and take leftovers. (Did I mention I was in full-time ministry?)

At the end of the evening when Don was behind the drum kit singing "Desperado" for the last encore, I wasn't in the crowd worried about traffic. I could be found sitting on an amp crate behind the horn section on stage. I could lean out and wave to sixty thousand people like I did at the opening of the new Mile High Stadium in Denver, and lean back. If security asked me what I was doing, I could point behind the drum kit and say, "I'm with him," and they'd say, "Do anything you want."

All of this happened not because of who *I* am but because of who *Don* is. Everything that is rightfully his, that he has earned, is bestowed on me because of my relationship with him.

Fast forward. (There's that cassette metaphor again.) One day God will be throwing a party in heaven that He calls the Great Banquet feast. It will make my sister's wedding look like a lousy roller rink birthday party by comparison. What we need to understand is that our ticket in is not *what* we know, but *who* we know.

We will stand before a holy and perfect God one day. If He asks us why He should let us into His heaven, will we just start quoting our Jesus trivia? "Well, God, I think there was something about walking on water, feeding five thousand, a baby in a manger, and some flying reindeer."

God will look at us and say, "I never knew you."

Or, when God asks us, "Why should I let you into My heaven?" will we say, "You know what, God? You shouldn't. I've fallen short of Your glory and perfection. I've missed the mark."

That's the definition of sin.

"For all have sinned [literally, "missed the mark" in the original Greek] and fall short of the glory of God." (Romans 3:23)

We don't deserve a seat at the banquet feast.

Further, Romans 6:23 tells us that the "wage" we earn from sin is death—eternal separation from God.

But, just when things look grim, we point over to Jesus and say, "But, God, I'm with Him. And everything that is rightfully His, that He earned—heaven—is bestowed upon me because of my relationship with Him."

In other words, I am covered in Christ, and God no longer sees my sin but sees His Son's righteousness.

"God made him who had no sin to be sin for us, so that in him we might become the righteousness of God." (2 Corinthians 5:21, NIV 1984)

"For while we were still helpless, at the right time Christ died for the ungodly." (Romans 5:6)

Not because of who *I* am, but because of who *He* is.

At that moment, God will look at us and say, "Well done, good and faithful servant" (cf. Matthew 25:23).

Isn't it time that—just like Don Henley went from the guy on the dusty CD on the shelf to the guy I say "pass the potatoes" to at Thanksgiving—Jesus goes from the guy in the dusty old Bible on the shelf to the God of the universe that lives in your heart?

In the end, will you be able to say, "I'm with Him"?

REFLECTION

....

Think about the famous person you would most like to meet. Is it a singer, actor, writer, politician? Keep that person in mind as you consider the following questions.

1. In spite of all you know about the person you pictured, if you approached them on the street would they know you?

2. Now think about how you approach Jesus. Does He know you? Sure, He made you, but have you let Him into your life, your whole life, or do you only approach Him when you need something?

3. What do you think it would mean in your relationship with Jesus for you to "put down your Jesus trivia" and genuinely have a relationship with Him?

4. Backstage passes, police escorts, fantastic food, and sitting on stage are the benefits listed about knowing Don Henley. What are the benefits you would list when it comes to knowing Jesus?

....

"Not everyone who says to Me, 'Lord, Lord,' will enter the kingdom of heaven, but he who does the will of My Father who is in heaven will enter." (Matthew 7:21)

"But to all who did receive him, who believed in his name, he gave the right to become children of God." (John 1:12, ESV)

10
Forgetting What's Most Important

· ·

YOUR FIRST APARTMENT. For many, it might happen sometime in college. Jerry Seinfeld suggests that your first apartment was when your parents would save the box a major appliance came in and let you play with it in the living room. You might cut a door or skylight, load up with a supply of Chips Ahoy and Capri Suns, and you were good for days.

Sophomore year of college was when I experienced my first apartment. And not unlike my high school English class, my roommates were a cast of characters.

Doug Allen: Doug was from the metropolis known as Siloam Springs, Arkansas. He wore button-down polo shirts and drove a brand new Corvette. Whenever a package arrived at our apartment, we figured it was a big box of cash from Sam Walton, the founder of Walmart. We think Doug was an early investor. His family owned the company that canned Popeye Spinach. If we ever found ourselves starving, we were set for spinach.

Andy Athey: Andy owned a pet hamster named Mother Teresa. If you fell asleep without locking your door, he would sneak in your room and jump on your bed with the hamster, yelling "Mother Teresa!" at the top of his lungs. He also referred to pretty much everyone as "Party Boy" and could do a mean impression of the Eagles' Timothy B. Schmidt singing "I Cant' Tell You Why."

Richard Davidson: To win $20, Richard once wore a green Speedo to the Baylor library and stayed for two hours. He had on a matching green polo shirt with the collar flipped up around his neck. I think that says pretty much everything about Richard. Cost me $20, but *so* worth it.

It was the fall of 1983 when the four of us set up our first apartment in Waco. Since the apartment was furnished, that just meant going to Pier One and buying a picture to hang over the couch and something wicker. It also meant calling the cable company.

Cable! Up to this point, none of us had ever had cable television before so this was a big deal. Television at this time back home in Dallas meant five channels. Flipping through the channels took about ten seconds. And by flipping, I mean getting up off the couch to turn the round "channel switcher" on the front of the TV. "Clunk, clunk, clunk." It was barbarian. Only the strong survived such cruel, brutal times (shudder).

Between college classes, I would often head back to the apartment for a break and a little magic of the thirty-seven channels cable offered. (Yes, I said thirty-seven. And at least sixteen of them were home shopping channels.)

MTV would be my first stop on the dial. Initially, MTV actually showed music videos 24/7, but early on there weren't many to choose from. After a few minutes of sitting through Ray Parker, Jr., singing "Ghostbusters" ("I ain't afraid of no ghost!"), the Steve Miller Band performing "Abracadabra" (apparently the only word that rhymes with the phrase "reach out and grab ya"), and witnessing Styx save the world from robots (*"Domo arigato*, Mr. Roboto"), I'd usually switch over to CNN.

Being an information junkie, I loved CNN. Back in those days, they did a new newscast every thirty minutes that often repeated stories. I remember one afternoon vividly. I sat mesmerized on the couch watching one particular story. I stuck around for the next half hour till they ran it again, as I was so struck by what I was seeing.

This story was about a skydiving filmmaker who was at the top of his craft. This was the guy you called if you wanted a skydiving documentary made or a unique shot for a James Bond type of film. He was the best at what he did.

This particular day, he was shooting a "tandem jump," which means he would be filming a student and his instructor, jumping out of the plane together. There were two doors on the small plane they were jumping from. One had the tandem jumpers hanging out of it, the other held the filmmaker.

The filmmaker had his camera strapped to his chest so you could see everything from his perspective. He jumped first, falling with his back towards the earth, so the camera shot back up at the plane. The student and instructor jumped next, in full view of the camera. They fell to earth for a while until the instructor pulled the ripcord, sending the parachute up into the clear blue sky.

Still free falling, the filmmaker rolled over, so his chest and camera were facing the earth. From his perspective, you see the earth grow closer and closer. Suddenly, the filmmaker's hands and arms start flailing frantically in front of the camera. Then, I heard the words that stuck with me. "At this point in time," the CNN reporter intoned, "our filmmaker realized that he forgot to put on his parachute."

Terror. Shock. Disbelief. And that was just me on the couch. I can't imagine the terror this man felt as he plummeted to earth without the one thing that could save him, his parachute. His camera continued filming, showing the ground rapidly approaching, and then everything went black.

The man died on impact.

But how could this happen? How could he have forgotten to put on his *parachute*??? What seemed so important that day that he left behind what was most important?

Being a film major in college, I think I may have some idea of what could have happened. He did have many important things to remember that day.

As obvious as it sounds, he had to make sure there was film in the camera. Back in the days of film, before everything went digital, it was easy to assume your camera was loaded, go out on a shoot, only to find you had to run back to the store. I've done it. And trust me, there are no Walgreens at 12,000 feet.

He had to make sure the battery on the camera was charged. There are no charging cables as you free fall to earth.

It was imperative that the tandem jumpers understood to let him jump first. If they accidentally jumped early, he'd be chasing them down, miss the shot, and they'd have to do it all over again. That's incredibly expensive.

He had to make sure they were over the right place when they jumped and would not land on a mall or someone's backyard.

He had many important things to remember that day, but none of them mattered once he forgot what was most important, his parachute. It didn't matter if there was film in the camera, if the battery was charged, or who jumped first, because none of those things could save him.

Can you imagine how he felt falling to earth going through his mental checklist realizing that none of those things mattered anymore?

I hope you never can. Although for most of us, it's easy to let the urgent take over our lives. Our to-do list can blind us to what is really important. There are bills to pay, degrees to get, jobs to do, and Joneses to keep up with. Even our relationship with Jesus can become a checklist. Read the latest devotional thirty days in a row, serve on that board, raise money.

We are not the first to let this happen.

Jesus told the church of Ephesus, "You have perseverance and have endured for My name's sake, and have not grown weary. But I have this against you, that you have left your first love" (Revelation 2:3–4).

"But Martha was distracted by all the preparations that had to be made. She came to him and asked, 'Lord, don't you care that my sister has left me to do the work by myself? Tell her to help me!'

"'Martha, Martha,' the Lord answered, 'you are worried and upset about many things, but only one thing is needed. Mary has chosen what is better, and it will not be taken away from her.'" (Luke 10:40–42, NIV 1984)

Get caught up in too many "to do" lists, and like the church at Ephesus and Martha, you'll wind up leaving Jesus behind.

Let me ask you a question. What do you think you are leaving this world with? A bunch of "stuff"? Perhaps a few houses, cars, wealth, and a few buildings named after you? Maybe you will leave with a nice and neat finished to-do list?

Like the filmmaker's list that day, none of those things can save you.

As Jesus said to Mary that day, "only one thing is needed."

Indeed, only one. A relationship with Jesus, the one thing that can save you.

As you consider these things, don't beat yourself up too badly if you find you've let the urgent take the place of what's important. Even Jesus' parents did it. (And they were in the Bible!)

"When [Jesus] became twelve, they went up there according to the custom of the Feast; and as they were returning, after spending the full number of days, the boy Jesus stayed behind in Jerusalem. But His parents were unaware of it, but supposed Him to be in the caravan, and went a day's journey; and they began looking for Him among their relatives and acquaintances. When they did not find Him, they returned to Jerusalem looking for Him." (Luke 2:42–45)

Too caught up in the details of life to remember Jesus? Take a note from some famous parents. Turn around and go back and get Him, just like Mary and Joseph did.

Unlike the filmmaker, it's not too late to grab your parachute.

REFLECTION

....

Take inventory of your life. What surrounds you? What fills your days? Reach back, like the filmmaker should have done before he jumped. What's back there? Have you forgotten anything?

1. What takes up the most of your time? Your worries? Or concerns?

2. Like the church at Ephesus and Mary, have these things in any way distracted you from a relationship with Jesus?

3. How can doing even "good things" become a distraction or a bad thing like Martha learned?

4. Who can you talk to in the next week or grab coffee with to discuss the priorities in your life? Is there someone who can hold you accountable to not getting lost in "stuff" or "to do lists" and point you to Jesus? Call that person and arrange a time to get together.

....

Not long ago, I attended the funeral of the father of one of my Young Life students. Charles Sammons died of lung cancer though he had never smoked a day in his life. He left behind his wife and four kids. On the front of the program for his memorial service was this quote from Christian author James Dobson that Mr. Sammons kept in his Bible.

> I have concluded that the accumulation of wealth, even if I could achieve it, is an insufficient reason for living. When I reach the end of my days ... a moment or two from now, I must look backward on something more meaningful than the pursuit of houses and land and machines and stocks and bonds. Nor is fame of any lasting benefit. I will consider my earthly existence to have been wasted unless I can recall a loving family, a consistent investment in the lives of people, and an earnest attempt to serve the God who made me. Nothing else makes much sense.

Charles Sammons was a man who remembered his parachute. We should follow his example.

11
God Uses the Little Things

· ·

INTERNET STORIES. The kind your aunt keeps forwarding to you. The face of Jesus appears in a grilled cheese. A left-behind family dog rents a car to drive cross-country to reunite with its owner.

The following story might sound like one of those forwarded stories. But just like Han Solo says in *The Force Awakens* when questioned about the Force, the Jedi, and Luke Skywalker, "It's true, all of it."

But unlike the Force (spoiler alert) this story *is* true. I was there.

We start with Kaitlin Seidel—cheerleader, softball player, full of life. As a sophomore at Pearce High School, where I was a Young Life leader, Kaitlin signed up for our annual summer camp trip to Frontier Ranch in Colorado.

After a fourteen-hour bus ride with all her friends, her adventure began for what we leaders had promised her would be the best week of her life. Young Life delivered on that pledge. Kaitlin laughed hard, did the ropes course, rode horseback, rappelled down the side of mountain, hung with her friends at the pool, and lived life to the full that week. Every evening, she sang loud at the nightly Young Life club meetings and leaned into the gospel messages compellingly presented by that week's camp speaker.

After a mountain climb—13,000 feet!—she listened to a message that night about how Jesus paid the price for our sin. For the first time, Kaitlin put it together: If she were the only person on earth, Jesus would have volunteered to die for her.

"For the wages of sin is death, but the free gift of God is eternal life in Christ Jesus our Lord." (Romans 6:23)

On a night like this at Young Life camp, every student is sent out into camp in complete silence, under the stars, to find a place to sit alone for twenty minutes and consider the message they just heard. Some nights the stars are so abundant and bright you can barely see the night between them. Some nights, it's as if God answers every young person's prayer for a sign, as shooting stars go off on cue. On cloudy nights, lightning strikes in the distance followed by the low rumble of thunder leave no doubt that the Holy Spirit—the "Hound of Heaven"—is on the move.

Well, He was undoubtedly on the move the evening Kaitlin stepped out under the stars. She was told a signal would end the twenty minutes, and then it would be time to head back to her cabin for a discussion of the message with her leader and friends. Some weeks the signal to return to your cabin is a bell, but this week the college and high school camp staff signified the end of the evening by standing in complete darkness on the dining hall porch, lifting their voices in song. The silence was broken as these words echoed against the mountain:

I'm forgiven because You were forsaken
I'm accepted, You were condemned
I'm alive and well, Your spirit is within me
Because You died and rose again
Amazing love, how can it be?
That You, my King, would die for me?
                ("Amazing Love" by Chris Tomlin)

As she walked back to her cabin, words of truth washed over and through her.

Her cabin's discussion time began. After the opening prayer by a leader, Kaitlin interrupted the proceedings.

"I have something to tell everyone," she exclaimed. "I just accepted Jesus under the stars!"

Everyone celebrated. Hugs exchanged all around. Tears.

Two nights later, Kaitlin stood up at the last club meeting of the week. Often a week of Young Life camp will conclude with a time we call a "Say-So." (The name comes from Psalm 107:2, "Let the redeemed of the LORD say so.") In front of more than four hundred of her peers and leaders, she said, "My name is Kaitlin Seidel, and I'm from Richardson, Texas. This week I started a relationship with Jesus."

Kaitlin's parents, Robby and Correll, said their daughter was beautiful before she left for Frontier Ranch, but when she got off the bus when we returned home, she was radiant. They knew something was different.

Kaitlin came to every one of our daily camp follow-up meetings, faithfully completing each one of her after camp devotionals. A brand new believer, she looked up verses in her new Bible, highlighted them, and prayed with her friends every morning.

Three weeks after we arrived home from Frontier, Kaitlin and the girls from her cabin decided to meet at Chili's for dinner before going to spend the night at their leader's house. Right there at Chili's, surrounded by her best friends, Kaitlin Seidel went into sudden cardiac arrest. Sadly, and within only moments, she passed away.

Unknown to anyone, she had a heart defect that had gone undetected. That night, her heart decided it could do no more.

Less than a week later, her three female Young Life leaders stood in front of over a thousand people at her memorial service and said, "A few short weeks ago, Kaitlin Seidel responded to the greatest love story ever, and we get to tell it to you now." And just like that, over a thousand people heard the gospel.

Kaitlin's devotional book she received at camp was found on the desk in her room. The page it lay open to was titled, "How Do I Know Jesus Lives in My Heart?" At the bottom of the page, in large, bright yellow highlighter letters, she had written, "Because I want to tell everyone about Him!!!"

Through Kaitlin's short life as a believer—only three weeks—she had just shared the gospel with over a thousand people in her unique way. But, God, the author of amazing stories, was not done yet writing her story.

Months later, on Kaitlin's birthday, all of her friends gathered at the Seidel house along with Kaitlin's Young Life leaders. The leaders invited her parents, Robby and Correll, to be adult guests at Frontier Ranch that coming summer. They wanted them to experience all that their daughter had experienced, to walk in her footsteps, and most importantly, to know the truth and hope that Kaitlin knew.

Though it would be difficult, they accepted.

Summer came, and the Seidels headed for Frontier with Kaitlin's camp scrapbook in hand. Their goal was to take a picture everywhere their daughter had so they could walk in her footsteps left a year earlier.

The fifth day at camp brought the same mountain climb of 13,000 feet which Kaitlin had hiked the year before. Robby, who is all of five foot two, cleans pools for a living. He drives a pickup truck as long as a stretch limo with a license plate that reads BIG ROB. Halfway up the mountain, his bad knees would not let him climb any further. Devastated, he had to tell Correll that he could not continue.

"You have to make it to the top! Kaitlin made it, and we have to get our picture there," she said.

"I just can't," Big Rob replied with tears in his eyes. He stepped off the trail to wait in the shade of the trees.

Correll continued on toward the summit. When the camp speaker for that week asked her how she was doing, she replied, "Kaitlin did it with a defective heart. I guess I can do it with a broken heart."

As Robby rested in the trees, he overheard a couple of older volunteer leaders who were also sitting out the climb to the peak discussing how they had lost their sixteen-year-old son recently to cancer. Robby's heart leaped as he made a beeline over to them.

"I lost my sixteen-year-old daughter this year!" Robby explained.

Hugs exchanged. Tears. An instant bond formed that only parents who have lost a child can know.

The couple asked Robby if he had experienced his first Christmas without her. Had he experienced her first birthday without her yet? They shared that on their son's birthday, they release helium balloons tied with birthday cards to feel closer to him.

Excited, Big Rob shared that on Kaitlin's birthday, the entire Pearce softball team gathered at their positions, leaving right field open for her, and released purple helium balloons in the air. Purple was Kaitlin's favorite color.

At that exact moment, Robby will tell you, a purple balloon came into view, making its way across the crystal clear Colorado sky.

Stop for a moment and consider that. The nearest "town" was St. Elmo, an old mining town, abandoned a century ago and over an hour down the mountain.

At ten thousand feet, on the side of Mount Chrysolite, God sent a miracle full of helium. He sent hope attached to a purple ribbon.

Descending over the trees, the balloon came to rest in a nearby creekbed. My friend Gail Akers scurried down to retrieve it, bringing it back to Robby.

"Robby," Gail exclaimed, "you'll never believe this!" She showed the purple balloon to Robby. It read "Happy Birthday."

Speechless, Big Rob didn't know what to do. In the middle of nowhere, literally on the side of a mountain, this purple balloon had just shown up. He emptied his backpack and carefully put the balloon inside and waited for Correll to come back down from the summit.

When she arrived two hours later, they began to descend the mountain together. Robby didn't say anything yet, as he was still processing what had happened. Correll, however, knew something was different as Robby cried the whole way down.

Why is he crying? I'm *the one who climbed the mountain!* she thought.

Later that afternoon I visited the Seidels in the adult guest lodge just to see how they were doing. As usual, all the adult guests were exhausted after the hike and were lounging around on the couches in the living room, completely wiped out.

Robby entered the room with his backpack. He carefully unzipped it, took out the balloon, and shared his story.

Again, tears. All around. Disbelief at first, followed by a genuine sense of awe and wonder.

Two days later, I had the privilege of talking again with Big Rob. As we sat in rocking chairs on the camp store porch, he shared with me that he was considering suicide. "If heaven is so great, I'd just as soon go ahead and be with my daughter," he said.

I shared that God had a better plan for him. I told him of the father God wanted Robby to be to their son Shawn. I told him of the husband He called him to be to Correll. Then, I got to share with him about the Savior who had already died in his place and who Kaitlin so desperately wanted her daddy to know.

"Robby, I think it's time you started your relationship with Jesus."

"What do I have to do?" he asked. "Do I have to sign something, say something at the meeting tonight? What do I do?"

"Do you want to pray?"

He grabbed me by the arm and said, "I thought you'd never ask."

We prayed. Everything changed.

Robby stood up at that night's Say-So, not far from the exact spot where Kaitlin had a year earlier. Echoing his daughter, he said, "My name is Robby Seidel, and I'm from Richardson, Texas. This week I started a relationship with Jesus."

The place exploded with applause. It seemed the entire camp stood in line to hug him.

I'm happy to say that the Seidels' story does not end there. They sit on the front row of their new church every Sunday morning. Robby is a greeter in their newcomers class. He decided if he is going to be a greeter he might as well dress the part. He wears a blue Walmart vest with the words, "How can I help you?" on the back. Correll was my son's children's Bible Study Fellowship leader.

The two of them have rarely missed showing up at their local Young Life club on Monday nights since that balloon showed up on the mountain. They are in the parking lot before every club, hugging and loving kids, remembering names, feeding the volunteer leaders and staff, and praying for the high school kids in attendance to come to know Jesus as they—and Kaitlin—do.

There are some days we may wonder if God can use us or our gifts. In comparison to others, we think we don't measure up.

"I'm not a great speaker."

"I didn't go to seminary."

"I'm not funny or good looking like that person."

"Their testimonies are compelling, and mine is dull."

We believe the lie that God only uses the "big" things.

Next time you are tempted to think something like that, remember this. Of all the "big" things God could have used in Robby's life that week—the amazing camp speaker, the hilarious camp entertainment, the 13,000-foot peak—He chose to use a simple 89¢ purple birthday balloon.

We have a God who delights in using the little things. Things like a little boy's lunch to feed five thousand or a borrowed donkey for His triumphal entry into Jerusalem.

I like to picture God as an artist. He's got His palette and the canvas He paints on. The Artist takes that purple balloon, the little boy's lunch, and a borrowed donkey to paint a beautiful picture of Himself for the world.

And if He can do that, He can also use your gifts. He takes a little bit of the smile you gave the baristas at Starbucks this morning, the better parking space you waved someone else into, the extra time you took to listen to your co-worker though you were running late, and the additional story you read to your kids last night. All these things He uses to paint a beautiful picture of Himself for those in your world.

And people lean in and notice. And respond.

The question is this: Will you be faithful in the little things, or just wait for God to use the "big things" to do the heavy lifting?

Oh, what we would miss out on if we thought God used only the big things.

"He who is faithful in a very little thing is faithful also in much ..." (Luke 16:10)

Every year the Seidel family gathers on the Pearce High School softball field and releases purple balloons for Kaitlin's birthday. And every year as the balloons disappear from view in the sky, Robby leans over to me and says, "Those balloons are halfway to Frontier Ranch by now."

REFLECTION

....

Think back on the things in your life that God used to point you to Him. What comes to mind? A great speaker or the kindness of a friend? A spectacular sunset or someone who took the time to listen?

1. Why do you think we sometimes fall into the trap of thinking our gifts aren't good enough in comparison to others?

2. What "little things" can you be faithful in today to help paint a picture of God for those around you?

....

Miracles are heading your way. Don't miss them by only looking for big things.

12
Pizza, the Apple Store, and Santa

· ·

GROWING UP IN THE SEVENTIES AND EIGHTIES, the mall was a magical place. If you could convince your parents to drop you off, it offered endless opportunities for new discoveries, mischief, girls (to whom I was too scared to speak ... until I hit my early thirties), and junk food. The food court was the United Nations of fast food. A stop by Spencer's Gifts offered a chance to ogle the latest *Charlie's Angels* poster and to pick up a Lava Lamp, fake vomit, or Pet Rock.

My first two jobs were at the mall. The fact that someone would pay me to be at a place all my friends were made me feel as if I was stealing money. We all worked at the mall and met at the food court for breaks. Plans were made for after work.

All my high school friends seemed to work at either Sanger-Harris, The Athlete's Foot, Sears, Joske's, or Paradise Bakery. The mall was the place to be.

The meaning and magic of the mall changed as I became a parent. When Michele and I had our first son, David, Thursday night around the Summerall household became "Daddy-David" date night.

Usually, by that time of the week, Michele was in need of a much deserved break while David and I were in need of pizza. Plans were made, the car loaded, and my son and I headed off to the mall. The next few hours were spent doing the things we liked to do together: eating pizza, exploring the wonders of the Apple Store, eating ice cream, and playing in the play area. (Spend enough time with me, and you will hear plenty about my four loves: the God who made us, my family, the greatness of Apple computers, and the Texas Rangers baseball team.)

Sometime around early November (or sometimes October!) a transformation happens at the mall: the Christmas decorations begin to go up. At our particular mall, no expense is spared. At the center court, a Christmas tree five stories high is decorated. Inside this specific tree is where Santa himself dwells. Every day he sits on a sleigh-shaped throne, greeting boys and girls as they sit on his lap making requests from their well-thought-out Christmas lists.

As David and I would make our way through the mall on these November nights, he would be drawn to the Christmas tree as any three-year-old would, mouth open, and with a sense of awe and wonder. Picture the Christmas tree as the Death Star (it was that big) and David as the Millennium Falcon being sucked in by its inescapable tractor beam.

Curious as to what was going on inside, David would take my hand and, trance-like, lead me to the opening in the middle of the tree and peer inside. Inevitably, we would find ourselves in line to see Santa, something he had never done up to this point.

Slowly, the line would move as each child got his chance for a picture with Santa. Some kids would smile and enjoy the exchange, like models from the Pottery Barn Kids catalog, while others screamed their displeasure as if going to the doctor for a shot. Each time the line would move, David would lean in and watch the exchange that was going on.

After a long wait, once we would get a few spots away from the front of the line, David would look up at me and say, "No thank you, Daddy. No thank you."

My sweet boy was just not ready, and that was OK. I was not going to force a Santa visit on my son. It would have to be his choice.

This scenario played out the same way multiple times. David would be drawn into the tree, we found our place in line, and then once close to the front, he would tell me, "No thank you, Daddy." Each time I would explain to David that it was OK not to see Santa and that we would get ice cream and hit the Apple Store (almost as magical as the North Pole) instead.

Later that same evening at home, he would request his mother and I read him "The Night Before Christmas" before he went to bed. He also wanted it read before every afternoon nap. That's twice a day for roughly fifty days straight. That's dedication. Before long, Michele and I had it memorized as we would patiently answer a curious little boy's questions about Santa.

Christmas grew closer as our Thursday night dates continued. One particular night in late December was different though. Oh, it started out the same. The tree would draw us in and then, hand in hand, we would find ourselves in line. This time, however, as we got closer to the front, David leaned in, closely observed a boy and girl on Santa's lap laughing and talking. David looked at me with wide and innocent eyes and proclaimed, "He's a very nice man." I knelt down and gently told him, "Oh, you don't know the half of it."

Our moment finally came as we made it to the front of the line and we were next. David had a decision to make. We could walk away and get pizza, or he could meet Santa. He looked up at me and then to Santa. The moment of truth.

He ran to Santa and jumped up into his lap. Santa gave him a big hug and tickled him under the chin. David laughed and then proceeded to ask Santa for a striped ball and a fire truck. Having read "The Night Before Christmas" every night for the past month at bedtime, David had seen Santa bring these toys to the little boy in the pages of the book. (He must have figured Santa had these toys readily in stock.) Hugs were exchanged, and a sweet picture was taken while Santa said he would do the best he could. David jumped down and waved goodbye.

Tears in my eyes, proud of my son's first encounter with Santa, I proceeded to the checkout to order the most expensive picture package to commemorate this occasion. I chose the one with two 8 x 10's, one 5 x 7, twenty-four wallets, tote bag, mousepad, coffee mug, quilt, a 3-D hologram, and an ice sculpture. He's heading off to college now as I write this, and I'm still making payments on that purchase.

As we were leaving, David's hand in mine, I looked down at him and asked him what he thought. He sweetly replied, "I love him *very* much."

David's journey to meet Santa is not unlike the journey we as believers take our friends and loved ones on to meet Jesus. There are people in your life you love very much whom you have taken by the hand and led to Jesus. It could be your spouse, kids, co-workers, or neighbors. Instead of a trip to the mall for pizza (though that would work, too), maybe it was a long car ride, coffee at Starbucks, or an invitation to church. Their initial response may have been similar to David's response to Santa. "No thank you."

In other words, they were telling you, "I like my life just like it is right now, and I'm just not interested."

Not deterred by this, however—and just like David and I didn't stop going to the mall together—you kept telling them the story and patiently and gently answered their questions. Perhaps their response to Jesus after a few conversations was, "He's a very nice man," to which you wanted to reply, "Oh, you don't know the half of it," as I did to David when he said that of Santa.

One day, though, like on that exceptional December night with David, we hope and pray that they will choose on their own to run to Jesus for the very first time.

We pray that one day they will be able to say of Jesus, "I love Him very much."

REFLECTION

....

Picture that person you most want to take by the hand and introduce to Jesus. Think through your family, co-workers, classmates, and friends. Begin to pray now for that person, that God would begin to break down any barriers that would stand in the way of them coming to know Jesus and one day saying, "I love Him very much."

1. Who came to mind first? Why do you think God laid that person on your heart?

2. Now, picturing that person, what would your version of "trips to the mall" be with them? What could you do to reach out to them and spend time together on a regular basis?

3. David knew I loved him and wanted to spend time with him whether he ever met Santa or not at the mall. Does the person you thought of know that of you? That you love them and want to spend time with them no matter their response to Jesus?

4. Reading "The Night Before Christmas" together gave us opportunities to discuss Santa and for David to ask questions before he was ready to meet him. Can you think of anything you can do

with the person you pictured that would offer a similar opportunity when it comes to Jesus?

. . . .

Take your friends by the hand. Take them to Jesus. Love them regardless of the response.

"But to all who did receive him, who believed in his name, he gave the right to become children of God." (John 1:12, ESV)

And if, by chance, you do get to hear them say of Jesus, "I love Him very much," celebrate. Stop by for pizza on the way out of the mall and get the most expensive picture package.

13
Outrunning God

· ·

A FUN TRADITION AT RICHARDSON HIGH SCHOOL was *The Senior Pub*. It was a book published each year made up of musings by the senior class. One of the highlights was a section where we made ten-year predictions about each other. In 1982, my classmates predicted this of me: "Ten years from now, Brian Summerall will be the host of the *Tonight Show*."

If you need to, go ahead and check the *Tonight Show* Wikipedia page. You will find that prediction did not come true. In 1992, Jay Leno took over the *Tonight Show* from Johnny Carson, precisely ten years after I graduated. Somehow I missed that they were holding interviews and taking applications. Sadly, there was no "want ad" listed in the *Dallas Morning News*, though I checked every day.

Before I was allowed a TV in my room, every night I would listen to *Tonight Show* host Johnny Carson's monolog via my magical clock radio with "TV Sound." I dreamed of moving to Los Angeles, practiced my Emmy acceptance speeches, and applied to the University of Southern California.

God pivoted my plans. In the fall of 1982, I packed up my Chevy Monte Carlo with my "Honk if You Love Brian" bumper sticker on the back and headed to Baylor University in Waco, Texas. Compared to Los Angeles, Waco was a vast wilderness. It proved, however, to be my spiritual promised land.

Walking into my first freshman "Welcome Week" session in Waco Hall, I found two thousand new freshmen standing and singing "Amazing Grace." The amazing thing that struck me at that moment was not God's grace; it was the fact that all two thousand of them knew the words. Every verse! Who were these people? I had no clue who this Jesus was that they talked about as though they knew Him personally.

With the help of a good high school friend, I finally came into my own relationship with Jesus early in my freshman year. I remember driving home one specific night and looking out the window of that Monte Carlo at the stars and saying, "I'm sorry, Lord. I never knew that You died for *me*. Thank You."

My Baylor days were spent hosting shows and reading the news on the school radio station. I produced TV shows, and made short films—all with my college friend Jeff Dunham, the now famous ventriloquist. (Turn on Comedy Central if you are not familiar with him. There's a 99% chance he's on right now with his friend, Achmed the Dead Terrorist. "I keel you!")

My Baylor nights revolved around Young Life—leading and playing guitar in local Young Life clubs, attending volunteer leadership training, high school football games, and Bible studies—as well as volunteering with a local church youth group.

I loved Radio/TV/Film. I loved my involvement in the Young Life ministry. By my senior year (OK, second senior year), I had a decision to make. Which direction should I go upon graduation? Long walks were taken across the beautiful Baylor campus for prayers about the future. Where was God calling?

The long walks always ended at a place on campus where a statue of Jesus stood. This particular statue was significant to me as it portrayed Him in the Garden of Gethsemane, face turned towards heaven, hands open, palms up, praying, "Not My will but Yours be done" (Luke 22:42). Jesus' posture in this statue said so much to me at this time in my life. His face was looking up to His Father expectantly, waiting for the Father to reveal His will. The way the sculptor portrayed Jesus' hands seemed to indicate He was releasing whatever Jesus Himself might want that will to be, opening Himself instead to what the Father wanted. That's what I wanted. These prayer walks I hoped would help me do the same: hold openhandedly what I wanted and look expectantly to what God wanted.

After many prayer-filled walks to that statue, I was led to full-time ministry with Young Life, leaving my other ambitions behind. I got my marching orders and, being the good soldier that I was, dove into Young Life immediately, first as a staff member in Waco, and then two years later in my hometown of Richardson.

Running hard, I dared all those around to keep up. All of this happened with the best of intentions: kids meeting Christ. What could be wrong with that? Nothing—unless you leave Jesus behind.

Fast forward through twenty years of ministry. The moment of truth came one December evening. Over the previous weeks, I had spoken at four Young Life fundraising banquets for other areas, led our own area's biggest club of three-hundred-plus kids and over a hundred parents, and preached at our church. I awoke in the middle of the night throwing up and could not stop. Soon dehydrated, Michele took me to the emergency room.

Once the revolution in my stomach subsided, the doctors ran a CT scan. Upon completion, the physician told me he was keeping me overnight for observation, explaining, "Your insides are inflamed and all screwed up." Good times.

That night started an eighteen-month journey of barely being able to eat or sleep. Bland turkey sandwiches, rice, and broth seemed to be the only foods that would not keep me in the bathroom all night. I "slept" in a recliner in my home office as it was close to the bathroom, and sleeping at an angle was supposed to help.

Sleeping didn't come easy. Each night seemed to bring a feeling of darkness more profound than the actual night itself. I couldn't push it off. The more I tried, the darker it got.

Losing thirty-plus pounds for someone who already had a slight frame (make that skinny) was a shock. Some thought I had cancer as my face was so gaunt. Looking back at pictures from that season of life is painful.

After over a year of living like this, I told my wife I needed to go on a spiritual pilgrimage, back to where it all began. I planned to drive down to Baylor and walk the sidewalks I used to walk, pray places I prayed, and finally, visit that statue of Jesus that had been so meaningful to me. Exhausted and at the end of my rope, I needed rest. I needed to hear from Jesus.

Driving the hundred miles or so south, I arrived at Baylor early one morning. First stop was Waco Hall. I sat in the seat where I first heard that version of "Amazing Grace" twenty-five years earlier. I could hear the voices, smell the smells. I walked the campus that day with a spirit of overwhelming gratitude for all God had done in my life there. The afternoon was saved for an appointment with Jesus, or at least my favorite statue, the one I prayed at and where I accepted my calling to go into full-time ministry.

Excited about what I might hear from the Lord that day, I headed to the location of the statue with great anticipation. Upon arrival, I was met with overwhelming disappointment.

Jesus was gone.

In the place where He used to be was a teenager dressed all in black, sitting on a bench, smoking a cigarette, reading a book.

I felt like Mary at the empty tomb of Jesus.

"They said to her, 'Woman, why are you weeping?' She said to them, 'Because they have taken away my Lord, and I do not know where they have laid him.'" (John 20:13)

My paraphrase of that verse that day might have read more like this: "Hey, punk emo kid! What have you done with Jesus??? And smoking, seriously? On the Baylor campus? Are you lost? And what's up with the black jeans? It's ninety-five degrees outside!"

But I digress.

In truth, I was distraught. The day was a failure. I came all this way to find Jesus, and He was gone. Literally and figuratively, I could not find Him. Lost more than ever, I started the long walk to the car.

Crushed, I called and told Michele I could not find Jesus. The eighteen months of darkness and feeling lost was now all summed up in one disappointing trip to Waco.

Driving down the service road by campus, about to hit the on-ramp to I-35 North back to Dallas, a building caught my eye.

It was the Baylor Alumni Center. I'd never been there before, but something in me was saying stop. Entering the building, I spotted a young college student behind the welcome desk.

"Excuse me, I know this sounds crazy, but when I was a student there was this statue of Jesus here on campus that meant a lot to me, and I can't find it. Any chance you know where it is?"

I described it to him.

"I know exactly where that statue is!" he replied. "You can walk to it from here. They moved it to the new seminary on campus."

He pointed, and I rushed out the door. After less than a minute, I spotted Jesus. He was a hundred yards away down the sidewalk, perched next to a new building. My pace quickened.

As I headed toward Jesus, I looked down at the sidewalk. Engraved into the concrete was this verse about twenty-five yards from the statue.

"You will seek Me and find Me when you search for Me with all your heart." (Jeremiah 29:13)

I had been looking for Jesus not only all day but for over a year.

My pace picked up even more as I headed His way. Ten yards from Jesus, I looked down and saw this second verse in the sidewalk.

"Come to me, all you who are weary and burdened, and I will give you rest." (Matthew 11:28, NIV 1984)

I was beyond weary and burdened. Entirely spent, rest is what I desperately craved.

Reaching Jesus, I fell at His feet and wept. I have no doubt the nearby students thought I was crazy, but this was a significant moment for me.

After moments in prayer in that same place I prayed so many years earlier, I felt God was saying something new to me.

Brian, I'm not your Baylor Jesus anymore. Years ago you got your marching orders and took off, but over time you left Me behind. I moved to other new things long ago and desperately want you to join Me there, but you can't if you keep looking back over your shoulder for Me where we started. I'm out ahead *of you doing new things. Look* forward *to Me, not backward.*

I nearly collapsed at this truth. In some way, I had left Jesus at Baylor. What part of "follow Me" had I missed in my desire to serve Him? I felt like Peter, Edmund, and Susan in C. S. Lewis's *Chronicles of Narnia* when only Lucy could see Aslan ahead of them leading the way because the three of them had stopped looking for him.

It was a process, but that day I learned to stop looking back over my shoulder for Jesus. I started to look forward to Him expectantly, excited to join Him in all things new.

"For I am about to do something new. See, I have already begun! Do you not see it?" (Isaiah 43:19, NLT)

I began to eat and sleep again. The dark circles under my eyes left. My marriage healed, and time with my kids was treasured once more.

God indeed led me to new places. I finally released the death grip I held on my Young Life Area Director job, giving up that position with no other job in sight. Once I did that, God created a new position in Young Life that didn't even exist before I gave up my old one. I traveled the country in that job, as well as Europe and Canada, training Young Life staff and volunteers. As a result, I participated in even more kids around the world meeting Jesus.

God had a plan. I just had to look expectantly forward and be willing to "jump" even before He revealed what it was.

I have no idea what's next. All I know is that Jesus does, and He looks forward with great anticipation to my meeting Him there.

"Follow Me!" (Matthew 4:19)

And when I don't, I pray He trips me again to remind me I'm not in the lead. He is.

REFLECTION

....

Take some time to remember when you started your current journey with Jesus. Picture the place, the people, the smells. Can you see it? Take a moment to remember what it felt like that day. Remember what you felt like He was saying to you at that point of your life.

1. Where have you left Jesus? Summer camp? In a church building? At the altar of your wedding ceremony?

2. Did you invite Him to the ceremony and walk out the doors and leave Him at the church? Did you accept the job or go to the college you prayed so much about and then leave Him behind?

3. Why do you think we can sometimes fall into the trap of "running ahead of Jesus"? Do you believe that we can do this with good intentions? Explain.

4. What steps can we take in our lives to make sure we keep Jesus ahead of us rather than looking over our shoulder back to Him?

....

"... let us run with perseverance the race marked out for us. Let us fix our eyes on Jesus, the author and perfecter of our faith ..." (Hebrews 12:1–2, NIV 1984)

You can't run a race fixing your eyes on someone behind you. You, too, will trip.

14
WHAM!

. . . .

LET'S TALK ABOUT TECHNOLOGY, OR THE LACK OF IT. It was once a big deal to have a built-in cassette tape player in your car. For those of you keeping score at home, cassettes followed vinyl records and preceded CDs.

Cassette tapes had two sides. You had to flip the tape over halfway through the album. Now, taking the time and effort to eject the tape, flip it, reinsert it, and hit "play" again was, of course, exhausting. (How did we get anything done in those days?) As a result, stereo manufacturers came up with the miracle of "auto-reverse." When one side of the tape came to an end, the cassette would reverse itself, saving you the trouble of ejecting and flipping it. It was magical.

Having a car stereo with "auto-reverse" quickly put you on top of the audio food chain. Having one in my 1981 Monte Carlo made me feel like the king of the road, or at least Cliffbrook Drive.

The cassette single (or "cassingle" as it was known) brought this magic to a whole new level. One song, both sides. The song plays, then you hear the "ka-thunk" of the auto-reverse, then the same song plays again.

What follows is the story of one such cassingle.

A young man attending Trinity University in San Antonio was dating a girl who attended Texas State University about fifty miles away. One evening before heading out to take his girlfriend on a date, a friend gave him the cassingle of the group WHAM!'s "Wake Me Up Before You Go-Go." (If you've never heard the song, take a moment to find it on YouTube. I'll wait. And, yes, the exclamation mark was part of their name. It was the eighties and we were all very excited.)

The sky was angry this particular evening as our friend drove. Taking a rain-soaked route that was off the beaten path, he unwisely took a curve at seventy miles an hour rather than the suggested speed of forty-five. He lost control of the car, flipping it, landing down an embankment sideways on the driver's side door.

Trapped between the steering column and his seat, the young man was unable to escape. The car engine shut off, but the car battery kept the car stereo playing.

The cassingle ("Wake Me Up Before You Go-Go") plays.
Then the "ka-thunk" of the auto-reverse sounds. The song
repeats. Ka-thunk. It plays again. Thirty minutes pass and no
one comes upon the accident.

An hour passes.

Ka-thunk.

Jitterbug ... Jitterbug ...

Ka-thunk.

*You put the boom boom into my heart; you send my soul sky
high when your lovin' starts ...*

Two hours pass. Ka-thunk.

*Jitterbug into my brain, goes a bang bang bang till my feet do
the same ...*

Four hours pass. Ka-thunk.

*You get the gray skies outta my way (do-do), you make the sun
shine brighter than Doris Day ...*

Six hours pass. Ka-thunk.

*Wake me up before you go-go, don't leave me hanging on like
a yo-yo.*

Seven hours! Ka-thunk, ka-thunk, ka-thunk, ka-thunk ...

*Wake me up before you go-go (ah), take me dancing tonight, I
wanna hit that high! (yeah, yeah, yeah, baby)*

Finally, after *eight long hours* of WHAM!-induced insanity,
the fire department and the paramedics arrive.

Paramedics lean down to the broken driver's side window
to check on the driver and are relieved see his lips slowly

moving. They lean in further and hear him quietly mumbling something.

"Eject, eject."

The paramedics reassure him, "Yes sir, the jaws of life are on their way. We'll get you out of there."

"No," the driver responds. "The tape. Eject the tape."

Later, doctors at the hospital report that if the driver had not been so irritated and frustrated by "Wake Me Up Before You Go-Go" playing nonstop for over eight hours, focusing on that instead of the pain, he probably would have gone into shock and fallen into a coma.

Yes, WHAM! could have saved his life. (*Jitterbug . . .*)

I so hope that story is true. Told to me by one of my former Young Life volunteers, he swears it is. Even if it's not, the principle remains true that what you choose to focus on during hard times is critical.

And, it can save you.

"In the fourth watch of the night [Jesus] came to them, walking on the sea. When the disciples saw Him walking on the sea, they were terrified, and said, 'It is a ghost!' And they cried out in fear." (Matthew 14:25–26)

Fear can make you cry out. Focus on it long enough, and fear can paralyze you.

Eleven men were paralyzed by fear that day. They were exhausted, hands bleeding, and scared of dying. Curses flowed freely. Traveling only three-and-a-half miles in ten hours against the wind and waves will do that to a man. Just think of the words you said in traffic yesterday. Multiply those by ten hours, then by twelve men, then add the possibility of death.

Fear, frustration, anxiety.

One man, however, chose to look past the storm and focus on something else.

"Peter said to Him, 'Lord, if it is You, command me to come to You on the water.'" (Matthew 14:28)

I've always found it curious that only one guy looked past the pain, fear, and bleeding hands. He took the time to see something different than the others did.

"And He said, 'Come!' And Peter got out of the boat, and walked on the water and came toward Jesus." (Matthew 14:29)

Eleven guys sat in the boat wallowing in their circumstances, misunderstanding what they saw, while Peter focused on Jesus. He rose above his present circumstances and accomplished something he could never do on his own.

Not that he was perfect, though.

"But seeing the wind, he became frightened, and beginning to sink, he cried out, 'Lord, save me!'" (Matthew 14:30)

Fear creeps in even when Jesus is in the picture. Jesus doesn't make you immune or oblivious to fear or storms. But, spend too much time focusing on the storm, and you just might drown.

When anxiety, fear, and depression get a foothold, just getting through the day feels as if you are under thirty feet of water trying to trudge forward (at times with a refrigerator strapped to your back, filled with bowling balls, injected with lead, just to make it a little heavier).

I kid, but I speak from experience.

It's easy to focus on the fear, pain, anxiety, and depression to the point that you stop looking for Jesus. And if we do, we just might drown.

"Immediately Jesus stretched out His hand and took hold of him." (Matthew 14:31)

Notice what Jesus didn't do. He didn't offer Peter a pamphlet on buoyancy or give him a book entitled *Forty Days to Flotation* to read. Jesus didn't offer him a program or hoops to jump through. He just reached out and offered Himself. And that was enough.

Not a complete fool, Peter grabbed the hand of his Savior. And so should we.

Reach out to the One who never lied to you. The One who, in spite of TV preachers smiling from the front of book covers, never told you there wouldn't be storms or that you can have "your best life now."

"These things I have spoken to you, so that in Me you may have peace. In the world you have tribulation, but take courage; I have overcome the world." (John 16:33)

No lies. You *will* have trouble. No matter how much faith you have or how much money you pledge to the new building program, there will be storms. Bet on it. Set your watch by it.

He did promise, however, that He will never leave us. He will be with us and get us to the other side.

"The LORD himself goes before you and will be with you; he will never leave you nor forsake you. Do not be afraid; do not be discouraged." (Deuteronomy 31:8, NIV 1984)

And that's enough. Because what you choose to focus on can truly save you. (*Jitterbug* ... Ka-thunk.)

REFLECTION

....

Take some time to stop. Breathe. Check your weather report. Where is the wind currently blowing? Are there storms on the horizon? Maybe you feel like you are currently drowning. Check your focus. Find Jesus just past the wind and waves. He's not far.

1. Where do you find yourself naturally turning when fear and anxiety creep into your life? Friends? Spouse? A bad habit? Something that numbs?

2. Where is Jesus on that list? If He's not first, then why do you think that is?

3. What habits can you develop during "sunny days" that will help you keep Jesus first as a place to turn when the storms roll through?

....

Make a list. Call a friend. Grab coffee. Share your list with them of how you will keep Jesus first on good days and bad.

And bring them a WHAM! cassingle as a thank you. If you can't find one on eBay, a cassingle from Air Supply, O-Town, New Kids on the Block, or Billy Ray Cyrus will suffice. You never know when it might come in handy.

15
Here's to the Crazy Ones

"I DON'T UNDERSTAND ANYTHING," my fifteen-year-old son said through tears.

"Anything?" I asked.

"Anything," was the reply.

It was his sophomore year of high school when David hit a wall. Diagnosed with dyslexia in grade school, we shored him up with every tutor and reading program we could. For years I had told him he was a "Mac" in a "PC" world, which is true. David's brain processes information differently than other people's. Teaching him the same way as every other kid is like trying to cram a Windows 95 floppy disk into a brand-new MacBook Pro. It doesn't work. (And who wants to be a PC anyway when you can be a shiny new Mac?)

Sadly, the one-size-fits-all private school which he attended since kindergarten did not see it that way. While nurturing, wonderful, and filled with inspiring teachers during his lower school and early middle school years, as you moved towards high school, the message received was that everyone must fit into the same mold. "Everyone must conform" could have been the upper school's motto. AP History and Honors English are the only options in high school. As I pointed out to the Headmaster, that is the equivalent of saying every kid has to play quarterback or play guitar in the worship band at chapel. It's not everyone's gift.

Unfortunately, my feedback was ignored by the high school that grades kids' prayer journals and Christian testimonies. (One of David's best friends received a 90 on his testimony. While it was still an A, I had to laugh when he exclaimed to David, "A 90??? Does this mean I have a 10% chance of going to hell?")

Question the narrow high school system, including AP History and Honors English, and the administration is happy to show you the door with a wan smile and say, "Our school is not for everyone."

Years of being a brilliant, creative, witty, square peg being hammered into a round hole had taken its toll on David. As he put it, "Eight hours a day is a long time to feel stupid." His shoulders were slumped over, confidence gone. If you beat down a kid enough by having everyone in the honor society stand, leaving only a few kids sitting, that high IQ kid will begin to believe lies about himself.

I thank God that David came to us. Some kids quit. Others act out. Some will try to numb themselves through drugs and alcohol. Sadly, others consider bodily harm. Even worse, some succeed.

David had a choice to make. Continue to allow this school to insist he conform to their way of teaching or leave all the friends he had gone to school with since he was five years old. To say it was difficult would be underselling it.

Enter a God who knew David long before he was born and who placed Michele and me in the right house before we ever had kids. One of the best schools in the country for students with learning differences, The Shelton School, happens to be within walking distance of our home. People move from all over the country to attend.

The only problem for us was a waitlist of five kids hoping to enter the sophomore class. It was the middle of the academic year, and six kids would have to move out for David to get in. The school told us that was not going to happen. On top of that, this was his only chance to get in—they don't accept juniors as it is too late to start their program.

Even though there was no room for David, the school agreed to look over his testing and make their recommendations for other programs in the area.

Then something completely unexpected happened during our meeting to go over our options. The conversation went like this:

Shelton Advisor: "We want David to come here."

Us: "You said you have no room and six people would have to move."

Shelton Advisor: "Yeah, but we think we can change his life, and that's what we get excited about."

Tears. Buckets of tears. That's what happens when someone believes in your child and throws a drowning family a lifeline.

One school says, "Our school is not for everyone." Another school says, "We'll move mountains to make this happen and change his life."

And they did. Winter exams were about to start at Shelton, so they told David to take an extra week off before Christmas break and relax. Additionally, we already had a spring break trip booked based on the other school's schedule, and Shelton's break was different. No problem. They told David to take two spring breaks. They informed us that time with family was more important than a week at school.

David made the brave choice to leave his friends and attend Shelton. His shoulders no longer slumped. He held his head high. The creative, witty sparkle returned to his eyes, and I recognized my son again. Instead of hours upon hours of homework and endless worksheets, he played guitar at a local Young Life club and ran his own business, earning enough to help buy his car. My son voluntarily showed me his report cards with a grin of pride and accomplishment on his face. And as promised, his reading scores drastically improved.

It's amazing what happens when a school's motto is "We teach students, not subjects."

I wonder if David's school experience is not unlike the experience some of us have with church. Like David, we feel like a square peg in a round hole on Sunday mornings. We believe we just don't fit in or can't measure up.

Author Donald Miller relates to that feeling in his book, *Blue Like Jazz*. "At the time," he writes, "I was attending a large church in the suburbs. It was like going to church at the Gap. I don't know why I went there. I didn't fit."

There are many reasons one might feel he doesn't fit in at church. Some are very simple, others more complicated.

—We don't dress the same, come from the same neighborhood, or have the same financial status.

—Whether real or imagined, we hear the whispers about our reputation or past and think we are being judged by the congregation or staff.

—Our learning/worship style is not standing for twenty-five minutes of singing followed by a thirty-five-minute lecture-style lesson. (Whose learning style is that, anyway???)

—Subtle (and not so subtle) hints from the pulpit suggest we vote differently than this particular church thinks we should.

Begin to believe the lie that we are not "good enough" to go to church, and you'll soon find yourself on the outside looking in. Author Brennan Manning shares a story similar to that in his book, *The Ragamuffin Gospel*.

> The story goes that a public sinner was excommunicated and forbidden entry to the church. He took his woes to God. "They won't let me in, Lord, because I am a sinner."
>
> "What are you complaining about?" said God. "They won't let Me in either."

A quick look at some of the characteristics of Jesus' disciples, and it's easy to feel you don't measure up.

- Careful students of Scripture
- Zealous and active in their stand for God
- Appetite for worship and prayer
- Consistent in worship and prayer
- Practice scripture memorization
- Not afraid of public prayer
- Active in the local affairs of the church
- Fast regularly
- Desire to stand against blasphemy and ungodliness
- Firm grasp of basic, foundational theological truths

Tough list to live up to. The only problem is that it's not a description of the disciples. That's a list of characteristics of the Pharisees who had Jesus put to death.

Here's a list of characteristics of the twelve disciples:

- Poor knowledge of Scripture
- Concerned for status
- Lack of courage
- Lack of commitment
- Dishonest
- Inconsistent
- Bad temper
- Frequent failure
- Confused
- Poor theology
- Prejudiced

(I have to give credit to the late Mike Yaconelli for those lists.) If you relate to the second list more than the first, you're in good company. Just open the pages of Scripture, and you'll find many far from perfect, rough-around-the-edges, square pegs in God's cast of characters.

Let me challenge you not to give up if you've found yourself feeling out of place at church. There are churches out there that teach about Jesus while letting you know it's "OK not to be OK." They are filled with real, authentic people who don't believe the perfect Facebook and Instagram images represent the reality and messiness of our lives. Take a chance.

David said making the decision to go to his new school was much harder than actually going to it. The decision to visit a new church is much the same.

Take a lesson from my son. If you are a square peg, don't let anyone pound you into a round hole. Risk. Step out. Visit.

Jesus refused to conform or settle for the status quo. So should we.

Here's to the crazy ones. The misfits. The rebels. The trouble-makers. The round pegs in the square holes. The ones who see things differently. They're not fond of rules, and they have no respect for the status-quo. You can quote them, disagree with them, glorify, or vilify them. But the only thing you can't do is ignore them. Because they change things. They push the human race forward. And while some may see them as the crazy ones, we see genius. Because the people who are crazy enough to think they can change the world, are the ones who do.

(Apple Computer)

REFLECTION
....

Think back on the stories of you know from the Gospels. Read the above "Apple" paragraph again, picturing some of those stories and how some people might have perceived Jesus then. Now think what would happen if He walked into your church today. Consider how He would be received.

1. How would you describe your current relationship with the church? Good? Estranged? Awkward?

2. If estranged or awkward, what steps would it take to heal that relationship?

3. What are you willing to risk to make that happen?

4. If you have a good relationship currently with your church, look around you next Sunday morning. See anyone "different" or maybe feeling out of place? What can you do to reach out to them and make them feel welcome?

5. If everyone looks, acts, and dresses like you do, what can you do to change that? Should you?

....

As my son walked out the door of his old school, the principal stopped him. It wasn't for a goodbye, or, "We'll miss you after attending here for ten years." There was no, "I wish you well at your new school." Instead he crossly asked if David had turned in his IBM Think Pad power cord.

In contrast, on the first day at his new school, David was given a shiny new MacBook to use. Coincidence? I think not.

16
A Christmas Trilogy

· ·

O HOLY NIGHT

I KNOW WHAT TO EXPECT CHRISTMAS EVE. Growing up, it was the day my grandmother, uncle, and aunt would arrive to spend the night. My Uncle Vance drove a long Lincoln Continental and owned a German shepherd. His car would roll into our driveway with the dog in the front seat and my grandmother and aunt in the back. That always made my dad laugh.

As the women made baklava in our kitchen, smells of Greek pastry would fill the house. Dad would build a fire, even if it was eighty degrees outside, while the kids would beg to open just one present on Christmas Eve. We never won that argument.

As an adult, Christmas Eve meant early afternoon church, dinner at my in-laws', and my sons begging to open just one present early. They've never won that argument either. Michele and I would put both boys to bed and then stress over whether we had the right batteries for each gift. A quick trip to 7-11 was not unusual to pick up a four-pack of D cells.

As I said, I knew what to expect. Sometimes, however, life interrupts routine. Sometimes, pain interrupts even on a holy night.

I spent Christmas Eve 2016 not in the way I expected. Tragically, my best friend of thirty years, Tod Bush, passed away a couple of days earlier as the result of a freak accident. While his brain showed no activity, his body was kept alive on a respirator for the last two days. You see, Tod was an organ donor, and his body was kept alive so he could serve as a gift to many with no hope. So on December 24th, I drove to the hospital for one final earthly goodbye and to try to find some closure.

Upon arrival, Robyn, Tod's wife, allowed me time in his room to pray, to tell him I loved him (which I regret not having said enough), and to tell him I'd see him in heaven. I left Tod's room and stood in the silent hallway. From a distance I watched Robyn through the small, narrow window in the door of the hospital room. She ran her fingers through his hair one last time and gave him a kiss on the forehead before he was wheeled away. All I could hear over and over in my head at

that moment were the words to the song I had just sung a few
hours before at church:

Fall on your knees!
O hear the angel voices!
O night divine.

Little did I know then what a truly holy night I was about
to experience.

Robyn and the kids (Tyler, Lindsey, and Kati) left. After a
long four days at the hospital, it was time for them to go home
as Tod's spirit had already "left the building."

I spent the rest of the evening and into the next morning
sitting with Tod's parents in the surgery waiting room as this
friend I loved became the ultimate gift on Christmas. The doctors began what is called "the harvest."

I was angry. I was sad. I was in disbelief as my best friend
was gone so suddenly. I wanted answers.

What I found instead was hope.

In the midst of pain and heartbreak, hope entered in right
about 8:00 in the form of a blue cooler rolling into the room.

It was accompanied by an EMT and two heart surgeons (one
in scrubs and one in golf pants and hat) from North Carolina.
They had just landed at Addison Airport and arrived by ambulance. One of the surgeons told us Tod's heart was going to a
woman who desperately needed it in North Carolina. While the

surgeons were rushed to the operating room with their cooler, we sat with the EMT for two hours and told her about Tod.

Next thing we knew, the EMT got up, the surgeons rushed by, thanked us, and told us everything went perfectly. Tod's heart rolled out the door in that blue cooler and boarded a private plane to North Carolina.

Jesus gave Tod a new heart when he accepted Him at Frontier Ranch thirty years earlier. On Christmas Eve, Tod gave that heart to a woman in North Carolina to save her life.

Love so amazing. Love so divine.

Within minutes, the next EMT rushed in with the lung team. We told her about Tod and his love of the Dallas Mavericks. We told her about the woman in North Carolina who would get Tod's heart and would soon be wondering why she has a strange desire to watch Mavericks games.

After about an hour, his lungs rushed out the door to save a man in Florida.

"Then the LORD God formed the man of dust from the ground and breathed into his nostrils the breath of life, and the man became a living creature." (Genesis 2:7, ESV)

The same lungs that God breathed life into for Tod would now give life to a man in Florida. The lungs that climbed mountains on Young Life trips so countless kids could hear about Jesus would now give life at sea level.

A thrill of hope, the weary world rejoices.

It went on all night. They took his eyes so a blind man could see.

Mary, did you know that your baby boy will give sight to a blind man?

He gave everything: heart, lungs, kidneys, liver, eyes, skin, bones, tissue.

Coolers rolled out, and planes took off one after another, filled with gifts of hope.

Tod gave everything so that people who had no hope on Christmas Eve would receive the gift of life on Christmas morning.

What's amazing about all of this and the reason it stirs our hearts is that Tod's story is God's story. What Tod did for so many that night, God did for all of us on Christmas.

Like the North Carolina woman's, God's Word says our heart is defective.

"The heart is more deceitful than all else and is desperately sick; who can understand it?" (Jeremiah 17:9)

We are in desperate need of a transplant. Without a donor, we have no hope, no life.

On that first Christmas Eve, God entered the story. But instead of hope in a rolling cooler, we find it in a manger. Hope entered the world in a baby. Jesus. God with us.

A world with no hope on Christmas Eve was given the gift of life on Christmas Day.

Jesus came that we might have life and life to the full (John 10:10).

And just like Tod, God gave everything.

"For God so loved the world, that He *gave* His only begotten Son." (John 3:16, emphasis added)

"Surely he took up our infirmities and carried our sorrows ... and by his wounds we are healed." (Isaiah 53:4–5, NIV 1984)

The ultimate gift.

"But to all who did receive him, who believed in his name, he gave the right to become children of God." (John 1:12, ESV)

Those who received Tod's gifts that night got a new life. Those who receive God's gift today get eternal life.

New heart, new breath, new sight, new life.

So that evening in the midst of heartache and loss, I saw God's story. I saw what God did for me. I saw hope.

I saw Jesus in Tod when he lived; I experienced Jesus in Tod when he died.

A thrill of hope, the weary world rejoices,
For yonder breaks a new and glorious morn.
Fall on your knees!
O hear the angel voices!
O night divine,
O night when Christ was born.

SING IN EXULTATION

....

THAT "HOLY" NIGHT DID NOT END when the last cooler containing Tod's organs went out the door. There was the long, tear-filled ride back home from the hospital. Streets are quiet and lonely at 2:00 A.M. Christmas morning. All is calm, but all was certainly not bright.

I pulled into the garage and walked through the quiet living room. Christmas lights on the tree and house were on. Stockings filled. Santa (my wife, Michele) must have visited while I was with Tod. I crawled into bed, waking Michele. She asked how it went, and I had trouble putting it all into words. Nothing prepares you for saying goodbye to your best friend, then watching his organs systematically go out the door to places unknown, to faces and bodies unknown.

Would they understand the gift they had been given? How could they know my best friend who gave it? They would not share our laughter, our inside jokes, our knowing smiles. They would not know the late nights of taking kids to camp, Mavericks games, and dominoes on Saturday nights.

Some may have slept in heavenly peace on that Christmas Eve, but not me. Not that night. I slept in an Ambien fog. I wanted to be numb. I wanted to sleep for days and find it was all a dream. I would wake, and Tod and I would be planning our next ministry endeavor, discussing our kids, planning the next night of dominoes, and picking our Baylor football season tickets.

Instead, I woke Christmas morning and went through all the motions. I have no clue what "As Seen on TV" gift I got from the boys or what I gave. I did my best to smile, knowing Tod's family would do anything to be opening presents with him that morning. I was determined to love, enjoy, and appreciate my family even more that morning.

One thing, one thought, kept me going. It was a song. (In case you haven't noticed yet, I'm a bit obsessed with songs and the places a lyric or melody can take you.) A song we sang at church on Christmas Eve before I headed to the hospital.

Sing, choirs of angels, sing in exultation,
Sing, all ye citizens of heaven above!
Glory to God, glory in the highest:
O come, let us adore Him,
O come, let us adore Him,
O come, let us adore Him,
Christ the Lord.

"Sing, all ye citizens of heaven above!" Citizens of heaven. They always seemed foreign and far off to me. Until now.

I knew heaven's newest citizen. I knew someone who was singing! He is singing at the top of his lungs, smiling that Tod Bush smile, blue eyes beaming.

I smiled. Tod hated singing. He loved music but hated singing. Before we took up playing dominoes with our wives and three other couples (for fifteen years!), we played random board games with our "Game Night" group. (I know what you are thinking ... these people know how to party.)

Tod was great at games and extremely competitive. That's why I always loved playing with or against him. The game he hated, though, was called "Humble." You chose a card and a category and had to hum a popular song for your team to guess. I took great joy in "humbling" Tod by always choosing him to be the one to hum a song. He would turn red, grit his teeth, and get it over with as soon as possible.

Singing "O Come, All Ye Faithful" with all the citizens of heaven that Christmas morning, Tod's teeth were no longer gritted, his face no longer red. It was radiant. It was beaming. He was in no rush, for he had eternity. Eternity to sing His praises. He was in the presence of His Savior, the ultimate heart donor.

Somehow I think Tod and Jesus shared a smile together. The knowing nod of fellow heart donors. Joy.

Because Tod accepted Jesus' free gift of life through His death on the cross thirty years before at Young Life's Frontier Ranch, he was "perfect and complete, lacking in nothing" that morning (James 1:4).

He sang and sang loudly because God keeps His promises.

"For as high as the heavens are above the earth, so great is His lovingkindness toward those who fear Him. As far as the east is from the west, so far has He removed our transgressions from us." (Psalm 103:11–12)

"Therefore if anyone is in Christ, he is a new creature; the old things passed away; behold, new things have come!" (2 Corinthians 5:17)

"He put a new song in my mouth, a song of praise to our God; many will see and fear and will trust in the LORD." (Psalm 40:3)

God is a worker of miracles. If He can make Tod Bush sing and actually enjoy it, you can believe He can make a new creation out of you.

I will never be able to hear "O Come Let Us Adore Him" the same way again. And when I do listen to it, I will look to the heavens with a smile for Tod Bush, citizen of heaven.

Save me a place at the dominoes table, my friend. I will be there before you know it.

GO TELL IT ON THE MOUNTAIN

THE DAYS AFTER CHRISTMAS. Eating leftovers, college bowl games, and trips to the mall returning gifts or buying that one thing you didn't get. After the loss of my best friend, I didn't feel like doing any of those things as the days passed after Christmas.

It's funny the things you remember and the images that come back to you following a tragic event. They replay in your mind as if you are trying to convince yourself it was all real. It's like a football game on TV when there is a controversial call. The coach throws a red flag and they go to the replay booth for review. The officials will replay the play in question over and over again to confirm what happened.

That's what I did for days, even weeks, after Christmas. My mind kept going to the replay booth and replaying what had happened that night to confirm in my mind that it was true.

There was one picture, one person who kept coming back to me. I could not get one particular EMT I met that night out of my head.

The role of the EMTs that night was to escort the surgeons from the airport to the hospital. Once the doctors removed the needed organ and placed it in the blue rolling cooler of hope, the EMT would rush the surgeons out the door and drive them via ambulance with sirens and lights flashing to a private airport and get them on the plane.

One EMT was different though. She refused to sit.

Other EMTs came and went with their surgeons and rolling cooler (all for Tod's organs, as we were the only ones there that night), but they all sat down on the couch to wait.

It's just that this one EMT refused to sit. She paced the hall, always on the ready, reacting to the slightest sound that came from the direction of the operating room.

She also refused for anyone or anything to get in her way.

She was more than ready when the blue rolling cooler with Tod's lungs appeared. With two surgeons in tow, she confidently but hurriedly rolled the cooler to the hospital emergency exit doors to rush to the airport. It was as if she were the entire Dallas Cowboys offensive line blocking for Emmitt Smith to run safely for one more Super Bowl touchdown.

There was one problem. The key card the EMT had to open the hospital emergency exit doors would not work.

From the waiting room, I heard her exclaim, "I don't care what alarm goes off. I'm kicking that door in, and we're getting to the airport!"

Bam! was the next sound heard. The cooler went out the door. I turned to Tod's parents and said, "That's the person you want carrying your son's lungs."

No time wasted. No excuses. She wasn't stopping for sandwiches on the way to the airport.

Take a step back. Can you see yourself in those pictures that formed like a puzzle in my head that week?

I hope we can see ourselves in the EMT. I think sometimes we don't fully understand what God is asking of us in the midst of a world in need of a heart transplant.

He's not asking you to be the heart donor. Jesus took care of that.

He's not asking you to perform the surgery. After all, He's the Great Physician.

He's asking you to be the EMT.

How? you may wonder.

He's done the heavy lifting, and now He passes the blue rolling cooler of hope to you to take to the world.

"And I heard the voice of the Lord saying, 'Whom shall I send, and who will go for us?' Then I said, 'Here am I! Send me.'" (Isaiah 6:8, ESV)

"Go therefore and make disciples of all nations, baptizing them in the name of the Father and of the Son and of the Holy Spirit." (Matthew 28:19, ESV)

"As for you, always be sober-minded [don't sit!], endure suffering, do the work of an evangelist, fulfill your ministry." (2 Timothy 4:5, ESV)

You've got your willing donor (Jesus) and a more than capable surgeon (God). Now grab the handle of your blue rolling cooler and take it into the world.

Go tell it on the mountain,
Over the hills and everywhere;
Go tell it on the mountain,
That Jesus Christ is born!

And be willing to kick in any door that gets in your way.

REFLECTION—O HOLY NIGHT
....

In light of Tod's story, take a few moments to reflect on God's story and His gift of life to you. Imagine for a moment the pain Tod's parents felt at the loss of their son and as the coolers headed out the door of the hospital. Now imagine God's feelings as His Son cries, "My God, why have You forsaken Me?" (Matthew 27:46) and He witnesses His Son's death on a cross. Finally, imagine the joy of the woman in North Carolina, the man in Florida, and the person who received new sight.

1. How do you think the woman in North Carolina felt when she received the call that a heart was ready for her on Christmas Eve? Do you think she delayed in any way rushing to the hospital? Do you believe that Christmas now has a special meaning to her?

2. Now consider the shepherds when they received the news of Jesus' arrival. "But the angel said to them, 'Do not be afraid; for behold, I bring you good news of great joy which will be for all the people; for today in the city of David there has been born for you a Savior, who is Christ the Lord.'" (Luke 2:10–11)

3. Read Luke 2:15–16. Did they delay or hesitate in any way in their response to the Good News of a Savior?

4. I saw Jesus in Tod when he lived; I experienced Jesus in Tod when he died. Who in your life helps you genuinely experience Jesus? Do you think anyone would say that about you?

5. At the end of your days, will you be able to say that you lived as Tod did, giving everything so that others might have new life?

"For I am already being poured out as a drink offering, and the time of my departure has come. I have fought the good fight, I have finished the course, I have kept the faith." (2 Timothy 4:6–7)

REFLECTION—SING IN EXULTATION

Picture those loved ones who have gone to be with the Lord before you as citizens of heaven, perfect and complete, singing in exultation in the presence of the God who saved them.

1. Who did you picture?

2. Now that they are made wholly new in Christ and in His presence would we choose to pull them away from that?

3. How can visualizing a loved one in heaven in God's presence help bring comfort to our remaining days on earth as we are separated from them?

"For I am confident of this very thing, that He who began a good work in you will perfect it until the day of Christ Jesus." (Philippians 1:6)

"... the dead in Christ will rise first. Then we who are alive and remain will be caught up together with them in the clouds to meet the Lord in the air, and so we shall always be with the Lord." (1 Thessalonians 4:16b–17)

REFLECTION—GO TELL IT ON THE MOUNTAIN

Picture God passing the blue rolling cooler of hope to you. Feel the handle in your hand and see the door ahead of you. Consider the direction you know He wants you to head.

1. When you grabbed the handle of your cooler and headed towards the door, what direction were you led to go? Family? Your workplace? A neighbor's house? A foreign country?

2. What are a few doors or obstacles that might get in the way as you try to head out the door? Fear? Opposition? Ridicule? Cost?

3. Will you turn around and go back to the couch, or are you willing to "kick in a few doors"? What would that mean for you?

....

May God say of each of us as I said of the EMT, "That's the person I want carrying my Son's heart into the world."

No time to waste. No excuses.

17
The Kissing Girls

· ·

GROWING UP, I WAS NOT EXACTLY what you would call "Mr. Social." My kindergarten playground was equipped with what became known as the "cool slide" and the "uncool slide." The cool slide was tall, shiny silver and red, and countless kids would line up to go down it during recess. The uncool slide was short, brown, and rusted. One of the bottom legs on it was bent, causing it to tilt. When you tried to slide down it, you fell off before reaching the end.

Every day in kindergarten at recess, I walked straight to the uncool slide and sat under it for the entire period, all alone. Not a great start to my social life.

By second grade, I had progressed enough to running around, playing games with the other guys. There was one problem, however, which manifested itself in a group of girls known as "The Kissing Girls."

Here's how it would play out. You'd be in the middle of a game and suddenly hear a high pitched scream (from a boy): "It's the kissing girls!" Immediately, a mad pack of second-grade girls would invade your game, capture you, take you hostage in the jungle gym, and proceed to take turns kissing you. It was a fate worse than death for a second-grade boy.

Sometime in late elementary or early middle school, you stop running from girls and might actually spot one you kind of like. You'd never dare talk to her but instead would write the all-important universal note. It usually read like this.

> I like you.
> Do you like me?
> Check one:
> ☐ Yes
> ☐ No
> ☐ Maybe

(I always added the "maybe" so if she wasn't going to check "yes" she had another option besides "no." It's all about the odds.)

Finally, to fold the note, you needed help. Sixth-grade girls can take forty-seven pages of ragged spiral paper and somehow fold it into a tiny triangle with another smaller triangle on it that says, "pull here." (I think this is how Ford folds airbags, using sixth-grade girls on an assembly line.)

Once folded, you wrote the girl's name on it and passed it down the row to her. She'd "pull here," read the note, and pull out her Bic Banana pen and check a box. Folding it back up, she'd pass it back down the row to you.

Sweating, you'd "pull here" in eager anticipation of the lifelong romance you were about to embark on. If she checked "yes," your day was made! You still didn't talk to her, but you were now officially "going together." Where you were going, you had no idea. You did, however, rub the note all over your face and sleep with it under your pillow. I had mine laminated.

And if she checked "no," you merely erased her name off the front of it, wrote in someone else's name, and passed it down the other way. At age eleven, there were plenty of fish in the sea, or at least in your homeroom.

It took quite a while, but as years passed, my social game slowly progressed. When I was twenty-nine, some of my Young Life kids set me up on a blind date with a teacher at their school. Friendship turned into dating and, next thing you know, we found ourselves looking at rings.

Michele was the dance team director at the high school, so when it came time to propose in the fall, nothing short of involving football and Friday night lights would do. I asked the school cheerleaders to paint me the ultimate note, a giant ten-foot high banner that read:

Michele,
Will you marry me?
Check One:
❑ Yes
❑ No
❑ Maybe

During the game, the cheerleaders unveiled the giant note. I climbed into the stands in front of the dance team. Dropping to one knee, I proposed in front of a few thousand of our closest friends.

Thankfully, the photographer for the football team caught one particular moment of the proposal, a frozen moment in time. I'm on one knee, Michele's hand in mine, but I still have the ring in hand waiting for Michele's response.

At that moment, there were many responses Michele could have given me.

1. *Saying No.* This, of course, would have been the biggest mistake of her life.

2. *Questions.* She could have looked at me and said, "This is great, but I still have a few questions. I really don't know everything about you—

"What did you make on your SAT?

"What was your favorite song in third grade?

"When was your last flu shot?

"Tell me more about these 'kissing girls.' How hard did you try to get away?"

Even after a year-and-a-half of dating, we still didn't know everything about each other. But, I wasn't asking Michele to pass a quiz. I was asking her to commit everything she knew of herself to everything she knew of me. Over time, we'd discover more and more about each other.

3. *Already Married.* "This is crazy, Brian, but I think we are already married. You see, you were born into a married family, and I was born into a married family. I think that means we are married, too."

After telling her she was nuts, I would let her know that a decision someone else in her family made to commit to a relationship does not transfer to her. She has to make her own choice.

4. *Emotions.* Michele could have just got caught up in the emotions of it all and stood there crying and saying how wonderful this all was, but never respond. I would still be there to this day, waiting for her to say "yes."

5. *Yes.* Finally, Michele could look at me and just say, "Yes." I'm thankful she did.

As you can see, a proposal requires a response. Just because I asked, didn't mean we were engaged or married.

The same goes for our relationship with Jesus. We have a choice to make. A response is required.

Jesus' friend Thomas learned this lesson in the twentieth chapter of the book of John.

"So the other disciples were saying to him, 'We have seen the Lord!' But he said to them, 'Unless I see in His hands the imprint of the nails, and put my finger into the place of the nails, and put my hand into His side, I will not believe.'" (John 20:25)

We all know someone like this. The friend that leans over to you in *Star Wars* and says, "You know, there's no air in space." Thanks, dude.

Thankfully for Thomas, something unexpected happened a week later.

"A week later his disciples were in the house again, and Thomas was with them. Though the doors were locked, Jesus came and stood among them and said, 'Peace be with you!' Then he said to Thomas, 'Put your finger here; see my hands. Reach out your hand and put it into my side. Stop doubting and believe.'" (John 20:26–27, NIV 1984)

At this point, much like Michele did on that Friday night in 1996, Thomas had a decision to make.

1. *Saying No.* Thomas could have said, "No, this is just too much," and walked out the door. Jesus, knowing love always requires choice, would not have tackled him and made him stay.

2. *Questions.* Thomas could have said, "I still have some questions," and still be there today asking endless questions—

"Was it really seven literal days in which You made the world?

"What happened to the dinosaurs?

"Can You make a rock so big that even You can't move it?

"Mosquitos? Seriously?"

3. *Already Saved.* Thomas could argue that he came from a good family who went to temple every week, so he had no need to make his own decision for a Savior.

4. *Emotions.* Overcome by standing before the risen Savior, he could just wallow in the feelings, cry, and never make a decision.

5. *Yes.* Or finally, Thomas could say, "Yes," just like he did in verse 28: "Thomas answered and said to Him, 'My Lord and my God!'" (John 20:28)

In other words, "Jesus, I'm in. You are who You said You were. Thank You for dying for my sin."

At that moment, Thomas was covered in Christ, washed clean of all sin.

And the moment we say "yes" to Jesus, so are we.

The Bible describes it this way: "This means that anyone who belongs to Christ has become a new person. The old life has gone; a new life has begun!" (2 Corinthians 5:17, NLT)

Maybe your spiritual journey is much like my social journey. Perhaps you've lived life for a while under your "spiritual slide," not interested in any of this "God stuff."

Then at some point, you may have heard or read something that piqued your interest in Jesus, and you thought, "I could run with this God thing for a while, but don't want to get too caught up in it"—not unlike my relationship with the "kissing girls."

But, finally, maybe even after reading this book, you realize the most significant love note ever written has been passed to you.

It's been forever written in the stars across the sky, in God's creation that surrounds you, and signed at the cross. The price paid was far higher than the cost of the ring I bought for Michele.

What will your response be? For, after all, when a proposal has been made, a response is required.

"... if you confess with your mouth Jesus as Lord, and believe in your heart that God raised Him from the dead, you will be saved." (Romans 10:9)

Unfold the note (God's Word). Let His love soak over you. Check "yes."

And unlike your sixth grade crush who may have checked "yes" to your note, talk to Him. He wants to be known by you and delights in your presence.

REFLECTION

....

Can you recall your first crush? Think back on notes passed down the row and those feelings of nervousness, excitement, and the anticipation of a potential new relationship. Reflect on receiving any of those notes and how that felt. Even if you never were passed a note in school, know that God has written the best note of all to you.

1. Let's cut to the chase. Have you checked "yes" to Jesus? (Notice how subtle I was there?)

2. It's been said that most people spend more time researching what movie to see or where to eat than they do investigating their faith. If you haven't checked "yes," what questions are holding you back?

3. Is there a mature Christian you respect that you could grab coffee with this week to discuss these questions?

4. Why are emotions not a reliable indicator as to what is true and what is not?

....

I said "yes" to Jesus for the first time while driving my 1981 Chevy Monte Carlo down Cliffbrook Drive one evening. You don't have to be at church or in the middle of some "moun-taintop" religious experience.

Do yourself a favor. Take your '81 Monte Carlo for a drive this evening, roll down the windows and say "yes" to Jesus.*

*Monte Carlo, evening, and windows rolled down are all optional and not required. A simple "yes" will do.

18
I Didn't Want to Leave

. . . .

IT WAS THE LAST DAY OF HIGH SCHOOL. Many mark their calendars and can't wait for that day. For me, it was a day I dreaded. I didn't want it to end. As corny as it sounds, I loved those people. I loved that place.

After that day in Miss Snodgrass's class when I finally came out of my shell, high school became my captive audience. Each class, each period was a new audience to try to make laugh. And the best part? They couldn't leave!

By the end of my senior year, I didn't want to give up my captive audience. Who would I be without them? What would I do?

As that last day of high school came to an end, I stretched it out as long as I could. I got out at 2:30. I didn't leave the building until 4:00. What did I do that extra hour-and-a-half? I roamed the halls. I did laps of A, B, and C halls, both upstairs and down. I stopped by every locker and every classroom I ever had.

When I finally mustered up the courage to leave the building, I made my way out to my regular parking spot and my blue 1981 Monte Carlo. I sat in the car and cried.

I gotta admit it's a bit embarrassing to recognize today, but I was scared. I had moved from the confines of that three-by-five box on the chalkboard in English class three years earlier to expanding my boundaries to the entire school. I didn't know if I could do it again.

Little did I know all of the stories that were ahead of me. God stories.

There were water fights to be had, girls' dorms to raid, and Eagles concerts to attend. I didn't know it then, but I would say "yes" to Jesus for the first time in that very Monte Carlo a few months later. My wife Michele and my boys, David and Daniel, lay ahead (way ahead!).

Yes, there was heartache, pain, and loss ahead as well. But those were all a part of the story God is still writing. And good and bad, they were all worth starting that Monte Carlo for and finally pulling out of that parking lot with tears in my eyes.

I was watching the *History of the Eagles* documentary recently on Netflix. (Yes, even though Don Henley is my brother-in-law, I still read every article and watch every documentary about the band I come across. Creepy, I know.) Joe Walsh, the lead guitarist for the Eagles and member of the Rock & Roll Hall of Fame, said something that kind of sums up the stories in this book and how they came together.

> You know, there's a philosopher who says as you live your
> life, it appears to be anarchy and chaos, and random events,
> non-related events, smashing into each other and causing
> this situation or that situation, and then, this happens, and
> it's overwhelming, and it just looks like, What in the world is
> going on? And later, when you look back at it, it looks like a
> finely crafted novel. But at the time, it don't.

I agree with Joe. Often it don't. But right now, it does. Chaos to calm ... at least for today.

I'm thankful there was life beyond Miss Snodgrass's blackboard and the walls of Richardson High School. I'm grateful for the stories God writes with our lives that reveal His truth.

"All the days ordained for me were written in your book before one of them came to be." (Psalm 139:16b, NIV 1984)

Thanks for letting me tell a few stories. There are more stories ahead, I'm sure, so I will do my best to move forward and trust the Author.

A final note: It's funny as I finish writing this book that Michele and I are having lunch with a group of my high school friends tomorrow. Donnie Boyd of YMCA/NASA fame will be there. We'll tell that story and laugh. The six foot four Swede, Bjorn Kirchdorfer, from Miss Snodgrass's class will be there, too.

And Candy Causey will be there as well. I still hope to make her laugh. Nobody laughs like Candy Causey.

I hope I made you laugh as well … and that I made you think a bit somewhere along this journey. Thanks for joining me for the ride.

ACKNOWLEDGMENTS

....

It takes a lot of help to write a book. I want to thank—

- Kit Sublett, my editor, publisher, and longtime friend, for his patience in guiding me through this process and for the many laughter filled editing sessions.
- Both the Bush and Seidel families for their friendship and for letting me share the stories of Tod and Kaitlin.
- Glenn Austell for the Monday FaceTime calls that keep me sane. Chuy's soon.
- My Young Life committee and supporters. The key to great ministry is to find great people and to grow old together. Thanks for sticking with me.
- My sisters, Vicki and Sharon, for their love and support over the last two crazy years, without which I would not have made it. Hilton Head, anyone?
- My college roommates and the crazy cast of characters from 3rd floor North Penland Hall for the nights of water fighting, dorm raiding adventures, and for giving me every excuse not to study. Sic 'em Bears.
- Michele, my lovely wife, for putting up with me and listening to these stories repeatedly for the last twenty-one years.
- My 1981 Monte Carlo, may she rest in peace.
- The Richardson High School Class of '82. We shared great laughs back then and I'm thankful we still do today. Much

love to you all and I can't wait for the next reunion! See you soon on the El Fenix rooftop. I'll bring the Virginia Rivers portrait.

- And finally, I'll finish the way I started: Thank you, Miss Snodgrass. Without you this book truly would not have happened. I was a skinny kid who needed someone to believe in him and you came along at just the right time. Thanks for the space on your board and for fanning the flames of my creativity. I can never thank you enough.

COLOPHON

....

Book designed by Randolph McMann for Whitecaps Media

Main body composed in Fournier MT Std 12/16. Fournier is based on Pierre Simon Fournier le jeune's eponymous typeface created in the 1740s. Titles composed in Neptune, a typeface designed by Gaetan Baehr and released in 2018

Cover designed by Jolie Guz

Cover image by Ryhor Bruyeu, Pond5

From manuscript to publication, every aspect of this book was created on Apple Macintosh computers